Who

Am

I ?

Who

Am

I ?

Ann Shaw

© 2021 Ann Shaw

First Edition: 12th April 2022

ISBN: 978-1-9993578-1-8

Published by "Who Am I? Books"

www.whoamibook.co.uk

annshaw@whoamibook.co.uk

www.annshaw.space

annshawspace@gmail.com

"Dedicated to my Final Teacher
Shri Ramakant Maharaj
who taught me everything
I don't know."

"After strong meditation and reciting the mantra, you will notice some changes. There will be less internal clutter because some of the illusory concepts, the garbage, has been removed. You will feel content and happy, extremely happy. There will be a kind of inner joy. This joy or bliss is not a response to something, but your natural state, flowing silently and permanently. There will be peacefulness. Even when you face unpleasant circumstances, this feeling of exceptional happiness and peace remains."

Shri Ramakant Maharaj

Contents

Foreword

Now is the time for the world to hear this Knowledge! I want you, Ann, to write another book, this time with the title, *WHO AM I?* Keep it simple and straightforward without any references and confusing Indian terms. It is my wish that this simple, powerful knowledge reach many more seekers, far and wide.

I want you to write this book in a popular style, for westerners, in particular. You know the culture. You know better. Use modern language with references to today's fast lifestyle, a society consumed by the internet and mobile phone culture! Frame the Knowledge in a contemporary way, so that the ordinary person, will be able to understand it! Make it light and fun!

Now is the time for the world to hear this Knowledge. Now is the time! This Knowledge is not the property of this *"Sampradaya"* (Traditional Lineage). It is "Universal Knowledge"! Make *WHO AM I?* simple and attractive, so that it becomes popular. This Knowledge is for everyone. We have to help others come out of suffering. We have to put an end to their suffering! It is our duty to show them how to wake up from the dream, and be free!

While we must never force this Knowledge on anyone, at the very least, we can try to make people aware! By presenting them with an alternative viewpoint, or a different way of perceiving themselves and the world, we can help bring them out of the illusion, and free them from suffering! All we can do is plant the seed, and then let the rest happen spontaneously. Whether they accept it or not, that's up to them. We cannot force them! So, go ahead! Go ahead!

Shri Ramakant Maharaj

Preface

Seeking ends here! *Who am I?* will finish your search once and for all. This book is unlike any other book as it takes you beyond knowledge. It contains the highest Teachings, which, combined with various Practices, will uproot all the illusion and establish you, in, and as, your true nature. You will be liberated from the mistaken notion you have of being a separate individual who was born one day, and will die some other day. When you realize your true, eternal nature, that you are not the body-mind, that it is only the body that dies, and not "you", the fear of death will spontaneously vanish, along with every other fear. You are unborn!

We look for happiness in the world, from love, relationships, sex, marriage, family, work, money, status, prestige, entertainment, food, alcohol, drugs, music, travel, fast cars, big houses, clothes, possessions, sports, books, art, religion, etc. None of these things can bring us permanent happiness. They can only offer us transient pleasures and temporary relief because they are all external sources.

This book shows you how to find permanent happiness from within. What you are looking for can only be found in you because you are the Ultimate Reality, the Source of happiness, peace and love.

I have been fascinated with the ultimate question, "Who am I?" for as long as I can remember. Feeling a little like an alien or misfit in the world, I spent a lot of time in solitude and reflection, trying to work out who I was and why I was here. In the early years, the Latin church services, particularly the devotional ceremony of "Benediction", mysteriously touched and transported me. Even though I did not understand a word of Latin, I felt at home in this beautiful, mystical atmosphere, filled with incense, bell ringing and gentle chanting.

Finding the meaning of life became, for me, the most crucial topic. Driven by a fiery determination and in hot pursuit of answers, I devoured as many books as I could. My interest and passion led me to the academic study of the subjects close to my heart, namely, theology, psychology, mysticism, comparative religion, etc.

Armed with intellectual knowledge and graced with several spiritual/mystical experiences, the search continued with a vengeance. The journey had its highs and lows - with long periods "in the desert" when I felt like giving up and abandoning the quest. But then, at last, what I was looking for, found me!

The simple and powerful non-dual Teachings and Practices explained in this book freed me from the illusory "I". My search was finally over! Your search can be over, too!

The world and everything in it is impermanent, but you are permanent, immortal. When this Truth is realized, you can live without cares, anxieties, worries and fears. Imagine being happy and at peace all the time!

It is yours for the taking! Imagine not having to keep searching because at long last, you know who you are! You will no longer need to listen to some of those ego-driven teachers who make their followers dependent on them! The beauty of this knowledge is that it is yours. You will fill the empty space you may feel now with your innate Knowledge, Wisdom and Truth, and not someone else's. If you follow the Practice, you will be guided by your Inner Teacher, the one and only True Teacher, that is your Source.

Why not embark on this beautiful journey back to Reality? Hop on the direct line to Self-Knowledge free of charge! You have nothing to lose, except all you imagine yourself to be, which is an illusion. You have plenty to gain: causeless, permanent happiness and peace!

Acknowledgements

With thanks to the incredible teachers of an
extraordinary, yet little known, Lineage – the
"Inchegiri Navnath Sampradya",
Especially, my Beloved Teacher, Shri Ramakant,
And His Teacher, Shri Nisargadatta,
Shri Ranjit, Shri Siddharameswar, Shri Bhausaheb,
and beyond.
Also, thanks to the numerous Teachers
who shined their light
to brighten the path Home.

Introduction

This book contains the Knowledge and the Practice that will liberate you from suffering and give you permanent happiness. Knowing that you are immortal makes you fearless.

A lifelong seeker, reading, studying, meditating, attending retreats, and banging my head against the wall, I eventually had the excellent fortune to meet my final Teacher, Shri Ramakant Maharaj. At our first "Skype Satsang", I told him I had always known that there is an underlying Reality. "Who has always known?" he inquired. His question silenced me. After a few seconds, I replied, "I don't know!" Shri Ramakant smiled. That moment was the beginning of my mind-bypass procedure!

I am indebted to my Teacher for what he used to call our weekly "Revision of Reality" during the first year when he encouraged me to keep going, keep "climbing the mountain". His loving guidance and enthusiasm were infectious and fuelled the journey's next leg. He always repeated the same thing after I had shared my latest experiences, saying, "Very good. I am very happy, but it is not Ultimate Truth. Don't stop. Go ahead! Go ahead!"

I am the editor of Shri Ramakant's book *Selfless Self*. (The late Alan Jacobs, President of the Ramana Maharshi Foundation UK, reviewed it, saying: "This is truly a great book and a worthy successor to the much-celebrated, Shri Nisargadatta book, *I Am That*.) Some time after its publication, Shri Ramakant instructed me to prepare another book, entitled *Who Am I?* He specifically asked for this book to be presented simply and directly, (minus stories or illustrations), to make the knowledge and the practice accessible to all. It has always been Shri Ramakant's wish to spread these Teachings, which he called "Universal Knowledge", far and wide, so that "many more seekers would emerge from the darkness of ignorance". After a series of unavoidable delays (by grace), it is finished.

Who Am I? is structured into six parts and divided into manageable, bite-size paragraphs for ease of absorption. The book investigates the root of our problems - our identification with the body-mind and all that we see in the world – and then it offers us a practical solution.

We need to undo all the programming and conditioning we have been subjected to so that we can uncover our nature. In the words of Shri Nisargadatta: "To know what you are, you must first investigate and know what you are not". When we have removed all the illusory layers and attachments, (such as thoughts, ideas, views, values, body/self-image, belief systems, etc.), through a process of elimination (*neti-neti:* "not this, not that"), then, what is left is our true Self, Selfless Self, that is nameless and formless.

Bootcamp (Part 4) introduces the reader to various practices that will dissolve our illusory baggage. (These practices are essential, especially in the beginning. First and foremost, you must remove the "thought-weeds".) Using the Practices of "Self-Enquiry", "Mantra recitation", "Meditation", and "Kirtan" will clear away all the body-based clutter we have accumulated over the years.

Parts 5 and 6 unite the head with the heart and knowledge with devotion. This is very much needed, as many teachers today share only partial, intellectual knowledge (without acknowledging the need for the practice of devotion), which is limiting. Here, devotion is to be understood as "non-dual". It is not devotion to an external deity, but to Selfless Self, which we are. As Shri Ramakant often said: "There is nothing except Selfless Self. Place your hand on your own head and bless yourself".

Traditionally, the two paths, of Knowledge (*Jnana*), and Devotion (*Bhakti*), have been viewed as separate paths, but they are really intertwined. Without them both, there is an imbalance. Following either the path of "Knowledge" or "Devotion" exclusively will not enable us to see the whole picture, the Ultimate Truth. The book ends with *Wedded Bliss*, the "True Yoga", where the longing for Transcendent Truth, and the longing for Transcendent Love, converge and unite in One Truth, One Love.

Who Am I? reveals the whole picture, the ultimate understanding, Ultimate Truth. If you absorb the Knowledge and follow the Practice, life will unfold spontaneously, fearlessly, and happily.

What you are about to read is fresh, direct and straightforward, but above all, transformational!

Let the alchemy begin!

~~~~~~~~~~~~~~~~

NB: These Teachings are beyond all words, concepts and identities. So, in this book, the words "she", "he", "her", "him", etc, are used interchangeably.

Part One: Who Am I?

"Everything that you seek, you are already that." Rumi

Chapter 1.
Who Am I? What am I?

The world is like a hospital filled with patients who are suffering from the same condition: chronic illusion caused by their identification with the body-form. We lost our way when a thick blanket of illusion covered over our Reality, trapping us in this material, transient life, with all its ups and downs, pain and suffering. The body-form is not our identity.

As babies, we were like brand new computers that were very quickly, steadily and relentlessly, crammed with more and more data. We were bombarded with one impression after another: thoughts, concepts, ideas, feelings, beliefs, suspicions, reactions, etc., which were all stored in our hard drives. As these illusory layers increasingly distanced us from our true nature, we began "living the dream"!

How the dream began

As you were growing up, you unconsciously absorbed everything you listened to and saw around you. You began to build your world and identity with this information, using body-based knowledge from the world of duality: success/failure, talented/untalented, positive experiences/negative experiences, positive self-image/self-loathing, pleasure/pain, likes/dislikes, and all kinds of self-talk. You were taught how to think, what to think, how to be and act, etc. This programming concealed your real identity. Inevitably, over time, one layer, after another, of your "make-up", in the form of thoughts, concepts and imagination, succeeded in obscuring your true identity.

And, in time, you forgot about your innocent and spontaneous nature; you forgot about your Essence. You don't know when it happened or how, but you know that at some point, freedom became a distant memory, a forgotten taste! Your new computer was no longer blank, but choked with a hard drive that was stuffed full of add-ons which had been uploaded and stored without your consent.

All this happened without your awareness. Once free and playful, the little child who loved to explore everything around her, with sheer wonderment and amazement, had vanished. Then the dreaded adolescent and teenage years followed. And before you had a chance, before even realizing it, you had entered the imaginary world, joining billions of others who were living within this circle of body-based knowledge. You assimilated into society the best you could. Once your identification with the body-mind complex had taken place, you grew attached to the known, operating within its familiar landscape, where life appeared to be safe and secure, for a time.

Your parents and relatives, teachers, peers, friends, employers, schools, places of worship and the media moulded you. One concept after another was firmly impressed on you. You accepted everything as truth. Why not? You did not know any better! These building blocks became your foundation stones and played an integral part in shaping and forming your identity. Before you knew it, your illusory life was in full flow. Your identification with the body-mind complex was complete.

You identified with your name

Your parents gave you a name, calling you Meghan, Harry, or some other name. As soon as you could, you identified with that. When someone called you, you responded automatically, like one of Pavlov's dogs. You grew up with your name, which has become very much a part of who you are, very much a part of your identity. But you are not that name, which like everything else, is an add-on. What you are in Reality is beyond all names! Who am I? "Will.I.Am" is the international music mogul and entrepreneur's creative response. "Will.i.am" is his trade name. Word-play is one of his many talents and hobbies, amusing himself and others as he conjures up all sorts of tricks with words - rhyming, rapping, etc. He uses language smartly and entertainingly; however, language is man-made; words are man-made. We all know that "will.i.am" is not who he is! The name given to you is not who you are either. "Will" is not to be found in words, and neither are you! No one can be!

Who am I? With social media all the rage, it often seems like the answer to "Who am I?" is a "Wannabe"! Everyone seems to be looking for overnight fame these days, either as a singer on TV's, *The Voice*, or a magician, dancer or some clown or other on the *X-Factor* and similar talent shows. But who wants to be famous? Who exactly is it who wants to be famous?

Who am I? An avatar on "Facebook" with 5K virtual friends? Maybe the answer to the question is a "selfie"? With hundreds of thousands of images scattered online, that could well be the answer. Sadly, the age-old, noble pursuit of examining the self is being replaced by a lifestyle of examining selfies on smartphones. Perfection must be attained before sharing these images on social media!

Narcissus, a figure from Greek mythology, was so impossibly handsome that he became infatuated with his own image when it was reflected in a water pool. Self-obsessed, he died from self-love, or so the story goes! The buzzing, selfie culture has recreated this kind of self-obsession to the nth degree. Everyone appears to be overdosing on self-love, selfies, memes - me, me, me, ego, ego, ego.

Falling in love with the dream

When you identified with the body-form and fell in love with the dream, your attachment to material things steadily, and relentlessly, grew and grew. The ego's addictions continued to expand so that the more you had, the more you still wanted. This bedazzling world offered you a massive variety of delights and desirables. "Want. Must have. Buy! Want. Must have. Buy!" Maybe you were surrounded by fellow consumers who were doing the same thing as you and climbing the material ladder. Witnessing this seemed not only to reassure you, but even encouraged you to keep going. They did not know any better than you. You followed the pack and became trapped in their web of illusion. Even when the monotony of it all (the job, the mortgage, the debts, and the stress of it all) was almost killing you, and you genuinely wanted to escape, you did not know how to get off the treadmill.

You have been fooled

This world has fooled you into thinking that you are a separate individual. It has tricked you into accepting that you were born and you will die. Your experience of the world with all its material, glittering attractions has trapped you in a vicious circle of unhappiness, stress, dis-ease, dis-peace and unfulfillment.

We are full of desires and never-ending wants and needs. But who wants? Who needs? These demands are made by the false ego, by who we think we are. The ego is never satisfied. When we have met our needs for, say, hunger, money, alcohol, drugs, sex or a brief dose of fame, the satisfaction gained is always fleeting. When unhappiness creeps in once more, followed by boredom, it's not long before we will start looking again for the next high. Seeking happiness from the material world has kept us on a hamster wheel, in a never-ending trap of wanting, having, and always wanting some more.

We are like children with zero attention spans, continually looking for new toys to play with and toss aside, play, then toss, play, and then toss! Never content, always restless, we are looking for something different, something new, something more. But the question is: Who is wanting more? For whom are all these desires?

Who am I? When you investigate and examine yourself, you will conclude that all these desires are for the ego, the false "I" you imagine yourself to be. This ego is a phantom. What you take yourself to be is fake and does not exist. Your self-construction has no Reality. You have been feeding a ghost due to your identification with the body-form and thought-forms. Up until now, you have been serving and nurturing an illusion - but not for much longer!

Full of hot air

The "I" you think you are, exists only in your imagination. When you stop feeding this false "I", the cycle of never-ending needs will come to an end. And when this happens, that "I", which struts around making ridiculous demands, will no longer be able to control you. The ego is the cause of your emotional roller coasters, and yet it is nothing but a hot air balloon. When that ego balloon bursts, all the other thoughts which arise to serve and inflate the ego-thought, will burst as well. And when this happens, you will be able to experience peace and contentment, at long last.

It is like you have been living in a house where the mind-ego-intellect had the upper hand and have been giving you the run-around. These three buddies always work together as a trio, dictating and directing you according to their whims. You have not been able to give your true nature any real or serious attention because the ego has been standing in the way, making endless demands.

The life you tend to take so seriously, this often complex and intense life you are so wrapped up in, is an illusion. Any and every transient thing is an illusion. This life is nothing but a long dream, a phenomenal appearance, whereby thinking, knowing and doing activities apparently occur. The thoughts, feelings and experiences are not part of your true nature because they are constantly changing. Using a method of "Self-enquiry", you will be able to get rid of the false ideas you have about yourself, such as being a mortal being. You will dispel the notions of being a separate entity or someone who is in charge!

Now is your time to wake up and discover your immortal nature. Embark on your greatest adventure ever to find "That", which never changes!

The dreamer's perspective

It is a tragedy to go through life asleep, never waking up from the dream because of our limited, uninformed perspective. You do not know who you are. To say that you underestimate yourself is itself a massive understatement. Because of the relentless pressure and conditioning you were under, you took the dream to be Reality and remained ignorant of your actual value. Functioning in the dark as a mere mortal gave you a narrow perspective on life, something like the following scenario:

"You have come to know yourself as a person called "So-and-so", of a certain or uncertain sex, who has lived for x number of years on this planet. You think you are the "doer" – every day, you get up, do this, and do that. The years pass by, often too quickly, as the monotonous routine of it all carries you along. You work, eat, and sleep. Some of you are single, while others are married, maybe with a family. You look forward to holidays with your family or friends, a break from the relentless, daily drill. Life is not without its pain and suffering. Sometimes you are happy, and at other times, you are unhappy, even depressed, but rarely, or never, do you stop to ask, "Why?" You handle it stoically like you handle everything else. Once you are on the treadmill, it is not so easy to get off. You just keep going and cope with everything as best you can.

You grow older… maybe fall ill… and then you die! Your body is cremated or buried, and then, after some time, a headstone is erected in your memory, saying something like, "She/he was a wonderful, kind soul…a bundle of laughs… may she/he rest in peace…". Is this the meaning of life? Busyness, job, career, family, friends? Is this who we are? Is this what our existence is all about?

Or maybe, if you end up in the hospital with a terminal illness, you will start scratching your head. It may only be then that you begin to think about your life and its meaning. You worked hard to take care of your family, and now, at only fifty-five years of age or thereabouts, long before you are even entitled to claim your State Pension, all you have to look forward to is an encounter with the Grim Reaper! It is so unfair! Angst-ridden, afraid and angry, you cry out, "Why? Why me?"

We are not what we take ourselves to be. The body-form is not the be-all and end-all; it is the medium through which we can know ourselves. We are not merely persons or separate individuals with needs and wants. We are not wives or husbands with families, jobs, mortgages, cars, etc., or single, unmarried or divorced persons! We are not individuals or separate entities at all.

You cannot take anything with you when your body expires. You cannot take your husband, wife, or your children with you. You cannot take your status or any of your treasured assets. Whether you are willing or not, whether you are ready or not, the time will soon come for you to leave the body with all its illusory attractions, possessions and attachments.

Reality's perspective

When you identified with the body-form, you grew attached to a temporary state. You are not the body-form. Wake up from the dream so that you can be remoulded and firmly returned to Reality, your permanent state, your original place, your Home.

You have forgotten your identity. You are not what you take yourself to be. You accepted the body-form as your identity and then went on to build your life, using illusory thoughts, concepts and your imagination. These concepts have moulded and obscured your true nature. When these layers of ideas and notions eclipsed your Reality, your vision was dimmed and became partial. You adopted the concepts of "birth" and "death" when, in fact, you are unborn - formless like the sky or space. You were never born; therefore, you cannot die!

Forgetting your true nature, you identified with the dreamer and the dream world. You realized "the false", "the unreal". To know ourselves as Reality, we need to reverse the initial process and undo the mistake; in other words, realize the "Real". Using discrimination and discernment, you can now separate the false from the real, fantasy from Reality, the permanent from the impermanent. You are permanent, whilst everything else is impermanent. Begin to investigate yourself, and then let go of everything you have accumulated, such as possessions, roles, attitudes, etc. All the things you have identified with are not you, and therefore, need to be cleared out. Underneath all the superimpositions lies the permanent, formless you.

What follows here is revolutionary, yet, ancient knowledge, universal knowledge. This knowledge applies to every one of us, the unbelievers, believers, atheists, agnostics, humanists, etc. Whatever belief system or ideology you may have identified with, or not, is of no consequence, totally irrelevant. Why? Because all these different stances have been learned and cultivated by the mind and the intellect. There is no such thing as an original thought. Your thoughts are not your thoughts. You adopted them from the position of perceiving yourself to be a body-form and a separate individual. They arose out of worldly, body-based knowledge, i.e., acquired knowledge. Your beliefs or lack of opinions, views or ideas do not matter.

In essence, we are one. Therefore, whatever position, belief, philosophy, religion, or political stance we adhere to, or not, has absolutely nothing to do with our true nature: Ultimate Reality. There is only One Essence.

You are immortal. You are not this body-mind complex that you take yourself to be; your Reality is formless. The secret is that you existed prior to the body-form, and you will continue to exist after the body-form expires. Are you ready to find this out for yourself? Are you ready to strip back the layers? Are you ready to demolish your imaginary house and then rebuild it on real and solid foundations?

Chapter 2.
Deprogramming

Remember those addition and subtraction tables the teachers taught us at school? Well, here, we are not going to add up anything. This process is all about subtracting, removing, and taking away our intellectual, psychological, and emotional layers of baggage.

Everything is inbuilt within you. You are the source of happiness, peace and love, so we are not talking about adding anything new. You do not need any additions or add-ons, as you are already complete and whole.

The veil of *Maya:* illusion, stopped you from remembering your true origin and goal when you were programmed to find meaning, happiness, peace and love in the wrong places. Instead of looking inwards, you set your focus outwards in search of self-fulfilment. You became addicted to the world, to others, to "the seen". The appearance of the phenomenal world sucked you in, distracting you from the fundamental goal of getting to know yourself.

Your Essence is, was, and will be, always. That invisible Presence existed before the body, the mind, the world, and the universe. You are before everything. The secret of your existence is already within you, buried under a mound of imaginary concepts such as self-image, ideas, beliefs, status, roles, accomplishments, etc. Undo everything that you have learned, which has conditioned you! You will not be able to know who you are unless the imagined you, the pseudo entity has been cleared out, removed, and swept away. Deprogramming is what's needed to return to the one Source that is our universal Home. This process is a simple one that involves the uncovering, subtracting, and removal of a lifetime's programming, until you connect with your true Self and touch base. Once you have eliminated all your illusory constructs, you can begin rebuilding your house, this time, on solid and perfect foundations capable of withstanding anything. The Reality Door will open gradually as you journey back to your original, Stateless State. Enter the portal to Self-Realization, where everything will be revealed. There, you will be able to tune into your very own broadcasting station and understand the true story of your life. Your story is everyone's story, as we are all part of that same, one, Universal Reality. Then you will be able to enjoy unlimited happiness and unimaginable peace - which is the real goal of existence - for free! No subscription or credit card number required!

When the Conviction arises that you are not the body-mind complex, the secret of your existence will reveal itself to you. The implications of this Conviction are not just far-reaching, but miraculous: an end to suffering, causeless, permanent happiness, and immortality.

Enlightenment is for everyone

Enlightenment means understanding. We will begin to wake up when the true knowledge of our existence is revealed. This knowledge will remove our ignorance and put an end to our suffering, once and for all. Permanent happiness and peace, a stress-free and fearless life, all of it can be yours!

So, who are we? What are we? We are one Universal Reality that existed before the body-form. We are one Energy, Power, Light or Source. It does not matter what you call it by, as our true, ever-existent nature is nameless, beyond language. We are that Essence that was there before the body, which will continue to be there after the body expires. It is here now as the Power, the Presence, that animates everything.

You are the central point of the universe. This is Universal Truth, the Reality that applies to us all, whether we call ourselves spiritual or non-spiritual. It does not depend on our acceptance. Whether we accept it or not, it is nonetheless the Reality.

Everything we can conceive of, or perceive, is an illusion, including spirituality. Spirituality did not exist before the body-form manifested. Spirituality's only purpose is to erase our misconceptions and remind us of our true identity. We have forgotten who we are. This knowledge is the cure for our amnesia, that's all. When it has served its purpose, you can forget about spirituality, or it will entrap you! Beware also of belief, faith and religion as they are also worldly traps that were non-existent prior to the manifestation of the body-form. Your Presence does not have any kind of language. Presence is! Presence is prior to terminology, concepts, spirituality, philosophy and every other discipline. You are prior to the term "God". The Presence is the Power, the only Source behind everything.

This knowledge is ancient Truth that has nothing to do with human-made philosophies and belief systems. What is presented here is your wisdom and knowledge, prior to book-knowledge; it is your innate knowledge - not something separate from you. You don't need to acquire it, you just need to uncover it, as it is already within you. Draw the curtain of layers of illusion and endless concepts, i.e., notions, views, opinions, stances, ideologies, values, etc., etc., which obscured your shining Presence and made you forget who you are!

Here you are not encountering something new. You are being guided to undo and remove the programming, the second-hand layers of conditioning, so that your inner fire, which has been lying dormant, can re-ignite.

You are Ultimate Reality, Ultimate Truth, which means that you do not lack anything. Nothing needs to be added to you because you already have the whole package. You are already whole. Your original nature is formless, without add-ons. However, to know this deep down and return home to your Source, your place of origin, deprogramming is essential. We need to erase everything we have accumulated since our childhood days!

Find out what you are not!

Our bodies are impermanent. We all know this to be accurate, but at the same time, we choose to ignore the fact and carry on as if we are going to live forever.

Who am I? Find out what you are not! You may think you know yourself, but you only know yourself as a body-mind complex. You perceive yourself to be a body with a head sitting on top of it, which contains the mind, ego and intellect. You are not that. You consider yourself to be a person, a separate individual. You are not that either. You have been living your life from this body-based perspective, always looking for a quick fix of happiness or a quick fix of peace. But the body is not your real identity. How can it be when it changes all the time? We are all aware that the body has a time limit, so, before your body expires, why not use a little of your precious time to discover your true identity? Give it some consideration, and then you will see for yourself that you are not really who or what, you think you are - a body-mind complex.

The body is a food-body

The body is nothing but a food-body. Whatever we put into one orifice must come out of another. The body needs both food and water to survive. If you don't eat, it will weaken and waste away. If you stop nourishing the body, it will eventually stop functioning. It is food that keeps the body alive.

The body is the layer, the covering for Spirit. You are not the body; you are the "sustainer" of the body. The body comprises five elements: air, water, earth, fire and ether, and is put together with some flesh, blood, bones and muscles, tendons, ligaments, etc. It is a messy affair. However, we are all deceived by its appearance. On the outside, it may look sweet and beautiful with its soft, delicate and smooth skin, but on the inside, it is not so pretty - a gooey, bloody mess!

The nature of the mind

The mind is not some separate entity but the spontaneous flow of thoughts that comes and goes. The mind, the ego, and the intellect are the body's subtle organs. When you say "my mind", this means you are not the mind. When you say "my intellect", this means you are not the intellect. "My" is not "I": you are separate from that. There was no mind, ego or intellect in existence prior to beingness. They do not have any power to function by themselves. Without your Presence, they do not have any ability at all. But they have been acting as if they are in charge of your life and running the whole show. Unwittingly, you have become their slave. Unbeknown to you, they have been living off your energy, sapping and draining you of all your vitality. The mind has no separate identity or reality of its own. The mind, the ego, and the intellect work together in this way: first of all, a thought arises in the mind, then the intellect processes this thought, until finally, the ego implements it. However, without the power of Presence, the "mind" cannot function at all.

When you come to realize that you are in charge, that you are not a slave of the mind, you will be able to reclaim your power and put these unruly squatters back in their place. You are not your thoughts; you are their witness.

Your Reality is neither the body nor the mind, but that all-pervading, still, silent Presence that you were too busy to notice while you were making your mark in the world. Unaware of your real nature, you took the body-form to be your identity, and in the process, you also accepted everyone else as body-forms.

You are the Witness

Your body goes through many different stages and changes throughout its life, whereas you do not go through any transitions. You are the one that witnesses all these changes. You were once a small child. That child grew up and became, say, a young woman, and then, an older woman. Throughout your life, you witnessed the child growing into a young woman. You are already - or soon will be – the witness to an older woman. The witness does not change. It is only the body that changes. You are the witness that is constant, untouched, unchanging, eternal. That which is changeless is unborn. You are unborn!

One day, whether you like it or not, the concept of time will come to an end and your body will expire! As much

18

as some of us would like to preserve our bodies forever, we cannot. Last call, or closing time, will come for us all, guaranteed! We must indeed leave behind our bodies and those of our loved ones, but we will never have to say "goodbye" to that Spirit or eternal Presence that resides in us all.

All these bodies we see around us will expire at some point or other, suddenly, or not so suddenly, due to medical circumstances or trauma, which could take anyone of us out at any time. But that Presence that we are, that eternal, formless, stateless existence can never terminate. The body's elements dissolve, nothing more. You are immortal. For you, there is no death, so don't worry, the undertaker is not going to take the real "you" six feet under the ground!

Death of the body

A famous affirmation says: "Today is the first day of the rest of your life". However, today could well be your last! Don't take anything for granted! Get to know who you are! Every moment of your life is an invitation to find that out. Don't leave yourself behind! You have a beautiful, unique opportunity to wake up from this dream and realize that you are not the body. So many bodies appear, and so many bodies disappear. Life in the body will one day end. Your body will go, but you are not going anywhere. There is no death. Death is a body-related concept. The great sages of all traditions have repeated this throughout the ages.

The body is limited, transient and finite. It has a time span, but you are not bound by time. You are beyond time and space: formless, unlimited, permanent, infinite and eternal. You are not the body. You were never the body. You could not be that. The body is not your true identity. This is a truth that needs constant repetition so that you can really hear it. You need to hammer this truth repeatedly until it is accepted and Reality is absorbed within you, wholly and completely. And when this happens, you will be free from all the imaginary shackles of fear, worry and despair.

Chapter 3.
Whose Bucket List?

Who am I? This fundamental question awaits an answer, and yet, this crucial, burning question is excluded from those popular bucket lists. Who are you? One of the many dreams on your bucket list? But to whom does this bucket list belong? Do you know?

You want to go swimming with the dolphins, or maybe you wish to visit the Himalayas, or even fly in a hot air balloon. That would be awesome! You may have travelled the world and visited many different countries, but have you visited yourself? Visit the visitor! Who is the traveller? Who is the visitor that is visiting all these exotic countries? Do you know?

You want to read the best-selling books, maybe the vast range of "Mind, Body Spirit" books, but do you know who the "Reader" is? Who wants to read these books? Who is the reader? You have not read the reader. Why not shift your focus and turn it 180 degrees around? Turn your attention towards yourself and go within. It is only by looking within, that you will find out who you are. Open your book and read your own story!

You want to live the dream. Reality TV shows abound, bringing overnight fame and success to the lucky ones, on Simon Cowell shows: *Britain's Got Talent, America's Got Talent*, the *X-Factor*, etc. At the same time, you remain unaware that you are already dreaming in a dream world. This life is a long dream. If you continue to seek out and expect your goals to be fulfilled by an imaginary world, you will always be disappointed. At the same time, you are adding more layers of illusion, and in the process, distancing yourself further from who you are, from the Source.

You may think you took birth on a specific day and will die on another particular day. And therefore, in between, you either feel that you must make the most out of everything, by enjoying life to the full - maximizing and squeezing every last drop out of it - or waste it completely!

If you want something, you must have it! You cannot stop yourself because the world has so much to offer you. You want to have it all! Look around you at those who appear "to have it all" and ask yourself if these people are happy, content and fulfilled? Research shows that while circumstances may improve for lottery winners, nothing really changes. If anything, they get worse!

Illusory thoughts and life-changing dreams have consumed us, such as, "What if I had a huge house, a luxurious home?" "What if I had power?" Or, "What if I became a millionaire, then I could go on a round-the-world trip, to Jamaica, India, maybe the Bahamas, etc., etc". But you do not know who this "I" is with all of its wishes. Who has all these fantasies? And from where do they come? All your wants and dreams are for the body-form which you are not. You are formless and vast with immense power. Your home is like the sky; your riches are beyond measure!

Your body is a shell

You may wish to have power and feel powerful, but you already have tremendous power, supernatural power, without knowing it. Without the power of Presence, your body is nothing but a shell, an empty vessel, a dead body!

You are the Source and Power that gives the body sentience, but you are not aware of it because you are unplugged and disconnected from the infinite Source.

You are a multi-millionaire with inbuilt, limitless treasures. However, you consider yourself poor, often dependent, needy, and sometimes, even crippled. Because you do not know who you are, you have reduced your status to a body-form with endless desires, really no different from the animal kingdom!

You may want to go on a round-the-world trip. Fantastic! All well and good; however, even if you knew the whole world, you would still not know yourself! Why not get to know yourself now! After all, you take yourself with you wherever you go. Look at you! Take a look inside. Take a trip inwards! Hop on the direct line to Self-knowledge! Journey within, and travel deep and still deeper. When you turn your attention inwards and search, you will locate the real you. You will find out that there is no other Source but you, that you are the Source of this world!

Selling yourself for passing thrills

There are very few truth-seekers because everyone seems to be having too good a time. How many even consider the fundamental question, "Who am I?" You don't seem to be able to stop for even one moment's reflection, but you will always find the time to look at your reflection in the mirror to check yourself out, smile, and give yourself the thumbs up, saying, "Oh, yes, I am looking kool!" before going out for the night! You are going out to have a good time. But who is going out to have a good time? You are not the body-form. You cannot take these good times with you. You cannot take your experiences, memories, selfies or anything else with you. There are no selfies on the other side!

The life you are living is a dream. Take this opportunity to see yourself, rather than mere reflections of yourself captured on endless selfies. Don't miss the chance to get to know who or what you are, while you still can.

Selfless Self

You are that energy of Presence without which you would be unable to smile, let alone take a selfie! You cannot see or talk without your Presence. Without Presence, your eyes, mouth, ears, etc., are just indents, holes in your face. Without Presence, you cannot do anything. Without Presence, the body is a dead body.

You cannot go pubbing or clubbing without Presence. Can a dead body go to the bar and order a shot of tequila? Can a dead body dance? You are not what you take yourself to be. Your smartphones will not help you discover who you are. You are not a person or a self, but a Self without self – "Selfless Self".

When we talk about the "self", with a small "s", this refers to everything that has come along with the body: the mind, the intellect, the ego, the senses, feelings, knowledge, identity, memories, in brief, all that can be conceived and perceived, which is false. When all this illusory, body-based knowledge has dissolved, then what is left is true – "Selfless Self".

"Selfless Self" is empty and free of content, free of illusion, free of an "I". Selfless Self is just another name for Presence, for one's spontaneous, invisible, anonymous Presence, which is beyond identification. While Selfless Self indicates our essence, Oneness, our identity beyond words, Self relates to our body-based knowledge and body-related illusions, such as, "I am somebody. I am an individual". There is no "somebody", and there are no "individuals". The self points to the identification with the illusory body: "myself", "herself", "himself", which is body-based knowledge, whereas "Selfless Self" indicates "no-thing".

Your Presence is within you, but you have not been aware of it because you have been giving your attention to the world. You have been neglecting Selfless Self. The visible is an illusion; the invisible, or the hidden, is Reality. Everything exists inside of you; nothing exists on the outside. The world is a projection of your spontaneous Presence.

Your Presence existed before beingness, and it will continue to exist after beingness. In between the before and after of your bodily existence, you have mistakenly accepted yourself to be the body-form and considered yourself as "some-thing". However, this perception is a mistaken one, a grand illusion! This world has fooled you into accepting yourself as a separate entity, an individual self. You believe yourself and everyone else to be individuals in the form of a woman or a man: myself, yourself, herself, himself, etc. There are no individual selves; there is only Selfless Self.

Always on the go

We live in a fast-paced world, a busy world, in which we are always on the move, with our large Americano or Latte coffees in hand, to get us from A to B. We never seem to stop. We are always going somewhere, attached to our constant companions, our phones, like zombies. Even when we are out walking or driving, we are on the phone, catching up, taking selfies, texting, or completing some business transaction or other. There never seems to be any time leftover so that we can just stop to catch our breath. There's no time to pause, to sit and just be. We are frequently in transit, constantly under the pressure of those seemingly important things that need doing: people to see and places to go! There's so much happening!

Stop! Touch base with yourself. Take some time out for yourself. Take at least one hour out of twenty-four to check in and catch up with yourself. Breathe! Be with you! Meditate and contemplate!

All your apparent happenings are taking place at the imaginary level. Nothing is happening! You are not doing anything; you only think you are doing all these things. Where are you going? Who is going anywhere? Catch your breath. Stop now! Today, not tomorrow. Take a look at yourself and contemplate the most fundamental question, "Who am I?" Take time out to reflect while you still can. Get off the treadmill! When the body expires, by then, it will be too late for you to find out who you are.

Chapter 4.
The Virus of Illusory Thoughts

You are not so different from your jam-packed computer which caught a virus that is difficult to fix. Your virus is called "chronic illusion". It is full of thoughts, concepts, feelings, misinformation, memories and influences, etc. You need to delete these infected files that have infiltrated your computer, as you will not be able to upload anything until you erase these corrupted files. This virus is infecting all your space to the point where you can no longer download, install, or update anything. It is just like having a notepad crammed full of scribbles, so completely covered, that there is no space left for you to write further!

"Presence" or "Ultimate Reality" is like your computer hard-drive. It is a perfect container: pristine, untouched, stainless and pure with infinite space. When we upload files to this container, we fill up the space like clouds obscuring the clear sky. These add-ons cannot affect or change our Presence, but they can overshadow everything. When "we see through a glass darkly", we are given an imperfect vision that confuses and complicates everything around us.

These add-ons in the forms of thoughts, opinions, feelings, views, beliefs, etc., are not part of who you are; they are not part of your Ultimate Reality. Over time, you have grown attached to, and very fond of these files, so much so, that now you are reluctant to remove them.

But they are not real because they were all acquired second-hand. All your carefully gathered data is deceptive. Find the courage to let it all go and click "delete".

Clean up your hard drive and make it blank again! Insert the anti-virus software and erase everything that's there. It should be empty, the way it was before all the worldly impressions left their mark on you. Delete all your body-based knowledge files. All of it must go because it does not belong to your true nature.

Truth does not change. Whatever changes - mental or material - is temporary and therefore, time-bound. If something passes, then it cannot be the truth. You have been giving all your attention to the worldly stuff and the changing concerns around you. You have been directing your focus to those illusory, pressing needs, but you have not given much attention to yourself. You have not looked at your true nature, at what you are, your Essence before the illusion descended upon you. We have been attending to the material and continually changing world while neglecting our unchanging Reality. In brief, we have ignored our invisible, permanent Presence, our Truth, our Ultimate Reality.

Remove all the add-ons

Discover what you are not! If you think about it, everything you have learned and everything you know to date is second-hand knowledge. It is hearsay, borrowed, acquired knowledge. If you try to say something, anything at all that you have not learned, you will soon find out that you cannot speak at all. You will be dumbstruck. Your true identity will reveal itself when you delete the many superimposed extras that are covering your natural Stateless State.

Contrary to what you may have imagined yourself to be, you are not the mind, the ego, or the intellect. You are formless Reality, pure Essence. Call it what you will! It is nameless because you are beyond words and worlds. You are beyond space and time. You are beyond the universe.

The "Invisible Questioner" is the answer

Who am I? The questioner is the answer. The invisible questioner is the answer. You are asking the question because you have forgotten your identity. The body-form is not your identity, however, it is the medium through which you can know your identity, your infinite Reality. The Real is not only stranger than you may think, it is stranger than what you can possibly think. The Real can only come about when all thinking ceases.

"Who am I?" is the only question worth asking because it lies outside the circle of illusory, body-based knowledge. Unlike any other question that we can ask, it does not have any familiar or known points of reference. When you ask this question, you are investigating your infinite Self, which is incomparable. When you pose the question, "Who am I?" you are enquiring after the enquirer. You cannot measure it against anything else that will help you reach a solution or find an answer!

When you investigate yourself and Self-enquire, you will find out what you are not. Question the questioner! Go within and find out what you are not! After uncovering what you are not, whatever remains is what you are.

Direct Knowledge

What is revealed here is not theoretical or intellectual knowledge but your innate wisdom. When your truth was buried under layers of illusion, you became blind to your Reality. But now, with fresh understanding and a recognition that you are whole and free, awakening and transformation can take place. You have always been free, but you did not know that you were because of the apparent obstacles standing in your way. You were imprisoned by darkness, without the light of knowledge to guide you!

Dissolve everything that was not there before the body-form! Erase everything that you are not. It is only then that you will know who or what, you are! Investigate yourself and contemplate on the way you were before the appearance of the body-form. As the unmanifest, you did not know yourself or anything else.

Duality began with the manifestation of the body-form. When Presence touched with the body, you began to know yourself, identified with the body-form, and started to believe in the illusion: "I am somebody". Your suffering began when you took that somebody, along with the imaginary world, to be your reality. However, with this knowledge, you will be able to discern what is false and reverse the process.

We signed the Contract

We signed the Contract with "Illusion" without knowing the T & C's (Terms and Conditions) of the Agreement. We sold out when we were tricked into embracing the body along with everything else. But now that we know better, a significant overhaul can take place.

You have lived as the body-form, under pressure of a multitude of concepts and experiences, since childhood days until now. And not only that, the force and influence of these impressions have caused many of you to feel anxious, fearful, even neurotic: "What if something happens to me? What if so-and-so dies tomorrow? What will happen in the future? What is happening in the present? What happened in the past? You may be worried about losing your job, falling ill or not coping. What if your close partner dies! What ifs... if only this, if only that, etc. You are always anxious about something or other. For many, anxiety has become a natural state, a comfort zone or default setting. Whether you are rich or poor, it seems to be the human condition.

However, despite this neurosis, somewhere inside of you, you know that there is much more to you, much more to life than your limited, and at times, angst-filled, daily routine. Meditating and contemplating on your true nature will put an end to the old scripts that have been going round and round in your head, like a scratchy vinyl record. Meditation, listening to the Truth, really listening and hearing it, accepting and absorbing it, will cancel the Contract and the whole illusory Agreement. You will then be able to see clearly, without any angst!

Amnesia

If someone experiences trauma in life and suddenly forgets who she is, she will be given some clues from past events, from close family members, to remind and help her recover her memory. She may be shown photographs taken of herself and her family so that these may trigger, register, and hopefully, help her regain her memories. If a child forgets something, the parents will remind the child. Similarly, here, you are being reminded of a long-forgotten memory: your origin and goal!

You also suffered a trauma when you were suddenly pulled into the world and alienated from your Source. This distressing event is the cause of your amnesia. You forgot about your essential nature that is blissful. You are not a woman or a man, but the Ultimate Reality.

When this knowledge triggers your memory, you will be on the road to recovery.

Hiding behind boredom

Maybe you have run out of finding ways to give meaning to your existence, so, after work, you need to keep yourself busy, and either go to the gym to workout or attend a class of Yoga or Pilates (and then go to the bar!). We put a lot of effort into keeping the body fit to ensure optimal health and keep our hearts ticking! That is important to us, but how much effort do we put into discovering Reality and finding out what makes us tick?

Sometimes you feel bored. You may call it boredom, but more likely it is a feeling of fed-up-ness, a cover-up and disguise for the emptiness and meaninglessness in life. Questions like, "What is this life all about?" "What is the point?" and "Who am I, really?" may be lurking in the background, just underneath the veil of boredom. But you don't wish to take on these big questions because you are not sure what might happen were you to look at them too deeply. We have all felt at some point in our lives that something was missing, but we would rather not admit this to ourselves. Many of us long for meaning, but we are too scared to alter our safe and familiar parameters. (Better the devil you know!)

When we pose the question, "Who am I?" we are not questioning a thing or an object about which we may know something - we are examining the questioner. At first, it may seem like we are just going round in circles, unable to find an answer. The question stops us in our tracks. We very much doubt that it can offer us any answers at all! After feeling as if we are banging our heads against a brick wall, some of us stop asking altogether. We conclude that it is a fruitless enquiry, leading only to frustration and sometimes insecurity, often leaving us more vulnerable and emptier than before.

We feel inadequate because we are not able to pin down an answer to the question, "Who am I?". We think we ought to know. There must be something wrong with us if we don't know! That could explain why many of us who have touched upon one of the fundamental questions of existence are too quick to abandon it and end up just burying it again. The question itself destabilises us, or if our egos are just a little bit on the large side, it makes us feel stupid. And, most of us would rather stay bored than appear dumb so, we close the door once more.

Forget about feeling stupid or insecure! Pursue the search for answers! Why? Because now you are on the most important mission of your life. When we ask this question, it opens us up to the "infinite unknown"! Nothing else matters more than finding out who you are! And not only that, the rewards are unimaginable!

The ultimate adventure

The shift or journey back to Source, from illusion to Reality, will unravel like a thrilling adventure, that is, if you are passionate about finding out your real identity. For this search, you will need to wear the hat of a law enforcement officer, so that you can track down the thief – the ego or pseudo "I" – responsible for committing identity theft. You will need a lot of determination to capture this thief as it is a clever one, a slippery culprit who appears in many different guises.

Unbeknown to you, the ego has been controlling your thoughts, feelings, behaviour, decision-making, etc. This false "I" instilled great fear in you - the fear of life and death. That fear of death haunts one throughout life. All you could do to protect yourself from every destabilising threat, was to attach yourself to something, to anything outside yourself - objects, people, material security, knowledge, books, family, alcohol, drugs, money, sex, beliefs, faith or religion. However, the universe will not let you hide for long, and so it keeps on calling you up! (The world sells "Life Insurance", here one finds "Life Assurance"!)

For those of you who have had a little peek and briefly contemplated the question, "Who am I?" you may have found the experience distressing. It was hardly an adventure! It is not surprising if stepping into the unknown scared you so much that you quickly put the lid back on! Fast forward a few years, say to a family crisis that forces us to question everything. Maybe you looked again, albeit briefly, but then decided it was best to turn away and remain within your familiar, safe landscape. Once again, you put the lid back on and continued with life as before like a loyal soldier, unconsciously trudging through the mud.

Now the universe is calling you again, offering reassurance that you have nothing to fear. Everything is an illusion! Intellectually, we may know that life in the body is a passing show, but at the same time, we do not live like that! Instead, we continue to prioritise the business of satisfying our bodily needs, munch, munch, gulp, gulp!

The knowledge that you are not the body needs to be fully accepted and entirely absorbed. It is only then that you will be able to loosen your attachments and dissolve the illusion. Self-enquiry leads to Self-knowledge or Enlightenment, which in turn, leads to Self-Realization. When you reach that stage, you will have little concern for worldly affairs. Your whole perspective will change; a complete transformation will take place. How will it happen? Through a deep and unwavering Conviction that the body-mind is not your identity. When this shift occurs, you will witness what is going on around you, observing the illusion, instead of being a part of it. With sufficient detachment from all the imaginary happenings, you will remain untouched, uninterested, uninvolved, and, most importantly, you will be at peace.

Chapter 5.
Take a Look at Your Photo Album!

Who am I? Give it some thought! The body has a beginning and an end, therefore, you cannot be the body. Take a look at the photos of yourself as you were growing up. Do you look the same now as that young child? Of course not! The body you see in these images has changed and looks very different. The body undergoes many changes from babyhood to old age, from the womb to the tomb! But you are not the body. You are changeless.

Who am I? You are not the mind and the thoughts. Thinking, feeling, perceptions, etc., all of these are in constant flux. Thoughts and ideas are for the ego, the false "I" or the small "i". When that pseudo "i" dissolves, the ego which has been controlling your life – let's call him "King Ego" - will be dethroned. And when this happens, thoughts and feelings will no longer hold any power over you. Your body is a material body. The "mind" merely consists of set ways of thinking and feeling that have become habitual. Your remoulding will take a little time and effort, as you have lived with these habits for decades. But eventually, they will all drop off!

When all the clutter has finally gone, "Selfless Self" will emerge as your permanent "happy place", overflowing with infinite contentment, joy and peace. Here is your sanctuary, where your beloved, closest, and most loyal friend awaits!

The ego is a hedonist

The hedonistic ego controls you and demands constant stimulation through the senses and the material world. The ego keeps the mind busy at all times, pursuing and fulfilling its desires in its quest for worldly entertainment. If you keep feeding the ego, it will keep demanding more. But when knowledge takes the place of ignorance - when you begin to starve the ego because you have caught it playing at its game - it will not be able to survive. The ego-mind cannot survive unless you feed it. When the light of knowledge exposes the darkness of illusion, the imposter will finally be revealed. And when you catch the thief that stole your identity, that illusory "I" will eventually be erased.

Escape

We live in a fast-moving world where we need more and more stimuli, props, support, escape and coping mechanisms to survive, just to keep the basic functioning going. The stress experienced by many is so intense that it needs an outlet, one as equally intense, to balance everything out! The need to let our hair down finds different expressions, with "excess" being the common factor.

The escape culture has gotten out of control. It seems that there is no longer such a thing as self-control, moderation or pacing oneself. Live for the moment!

Beer, shots, wine... heroin, ecstasy, etc. There is a considerable choice readily available for all! Drinking and partying too much, while living *La Vida Loca* means not caring about the consequences. It sometimes seems that the main driving force or only intention, is to fill the void.

From what are we escaping? A monotonous life that we find boring, empty and meaningless? There may be reasons for the excess, such as trying to numb uncomfortable feelings, relationship problems and tensions, break-ups, loneliness, etc. Then again, it sometimes seems that many of us don't need a reason. Perhaps we are going through something like a semi-permanent or permanent existential crisis!

Feelings of depression, anxiety, loneliness, and inadequacy affect us more and more, exacerbated by the 24/7 online culture. There is no escape from the immense pressures of social media which scrutinize everyone!

Witness the movie

All the thoughts and feelings that you experience are bodily feelings, like waves that come and go. You are not part of all that. The real you is rooted, anchored, steady and immovable. Try viewing all that appears to be happening in the same way as, say, if you were at the cinema. While you are watching a movie, you sometimes laugh, and you sometimes cry.

Similarly, what you see in life is a movie that you are projecting. Try observing the moving images without identifying with them. Just witness the film. The world, as you see it, is your projection. Don't let the mind play with you, telling you otherwise. The mind is separate from you. You have nothing to do with it; you are nothing to do with it.

Observe the ego's behaviour. When it gets what it needs from an external object, it is happy for a while. However, if it does not get its needs met, there are tantrums, anger, anxiety, fear, and even despair. Both positive and negative emotions, including happiness, are illusory because they come from a make-believe world that serves the false ego's needs. You are like the hamster, going round and round the wheel, following every desire. Realize that material objects cannot satisfy you, and no matter how hard you try, they will never be able to fulfil you! How can anything that is time-bound bring you permanent happiness?

The "I" you think you are is not you! This is the crux of the matter! You are not a limited, bodily being but a non-material, Spirit Being. You are an unlimited being that will only find fulfilment and happiness from your most intimate "I" which is your Spiritual Heart, the Supreme Self, your Source within, Selfless Self, which is the nameless core of your existence. All your unhappiness arises from taking what you see to be Reality, when in fact, it is only a reflection, a shadow. The seen is not your Reality; the Seer is Reality. Shift your focus and cultivate staying with the Seer, your permanent essential nature, instead of the seen which is temporary. How do you do this? By developing the "Witness" attitude, you will be able to disidentify from the thoughts, perceptions, emotions, desires, etc. Ultimately, your detachment and observation of these distracting fluctuations will prevent upsets, unhappiness, and suffering.

When you have cleaned the slate and know, who or what you are, happiness and peace will surge within. You will learn to dance through life because the pseudo ego that was controlling you has now vanished, liberating you to live freely and spontaneously!

Chapter 6.
Consumed by the Material World

Many of us live our lives sleep-walking through this long dream of life. We wonder why, most of the time we are not happy! We depend on external things and others to make us happy and keep us happy. The human condition with its ups and downs, pain and suffering is intolerable, so we keep looking for distractions, an escape, something to pass the time - anything to dull the senses, or excite the senses.

A safe and secure life is a dry life. Maybe you have already worn the various T-shirts, climbed the career ladder, had a husband or wife and kids. Perhaps you are going through a midlife crisis, and you wonder, "What next?" What was the meaning of it all?"

Who am I? What is behind, underneath it all? What is your true identity? Find out! This kind of self-questioning is called Self-enquiry. Why should you bother? So that you can find peace! And who doesn't want peace? When you investigate yourself and apply discrimination and discernment, you will identify all the add-ons to your original, Stateless State. Once you have recognised these, you can disidentify from their influences: various thought patterns, fixed ideas, misconceptions, perceptions, etc., and overcome them. The practice of Self-enquiry will help you to detach from your habits, coping mechanisms and survival tools. It will lead you to Self-knowledge, where you will begin to live life authentically from your authentic centre, by just being as you are. You will start to live life easily and stress-free when you let go of the false, of everything that does not belong to you, of everything that is not real.

Why is Self-enquiry useful? Because it helps us to discriminate between Reality and illusion. When you separate Reality from illusion, you will be able to let go of the attachments that have imprisoned you throughout life and kept you small. You will be able to see yourself as you truly are: transcendent, free, shining, limitless, eternal!

Fear

Our intense fear of death accompanies our strong desire and determination to live. Most of us fear death and thus cannot love and live life fully. When we think or believe that something is real such as death, we experience fear, pain and suffering. We are afraid to die, scared of the unknown, and fearful of annihilation. The thought of no longer existing can evoke an unbearable sense of dread and terror. However, when you understand that the "True You" is indestructible, that there is no death, then you will no longer be submerged by these conceptual traps of fear and death.

The long dream

Caught up in the long dream of life, you often regret the past, or worry about the future. There is no "past", "future", or "present". These are only concepts. Your problems appear to be significant because you give so much importance to the body-form's dream, which is an illusion. It is like one of your bad dreams in which you appear to be struggling with someone, and then, suddenly, when you wake up, you are relieved because the struggle has ended, often saying, "Thank God, it was only a dream!" This life is that dream!

For the most part, you don't take your dreams seriously; you don't own them. You can forget about them. Similarly, you don't have to buy into this dream life and allow the world to drag you down. Take a step back and distance yourself from all that is going on around you, so that you can witness and observe the scenery. That witness remains untouched and unscathed because it knows that it is "in the world, but not of the world".

Don't cling to this material life. Let go of your attachments. Wake up now and find out who you are! You have a fantastic opportunity to use the body-form as the vehicle it was meant for: to find your origin, find your goal! It is your "get out of jail card", your freedom pass. Don't miss out! Come out of all this illusion and get to know who you are!

Waking up from the coma

Awakening means that you genuinely know who you are, and you hold the Conviction that you are not just this body-form. You need to hammer home this truth until it is established. When this happens, you will no longer be so interested in the world or drawn to its appearances. If you keep giving too much attention to external things, there will always be problems.

The truth of your existence is that you are the Ultimate Reality. Whether you accept this or not is entirely up to you. You can carry on as you are, sometimes partying with the dream of life, and at other times, struggling with its nightmare. Or, you can wake up from the coma, Self-realize and party in Reality!

It is a tragedy to go through life in a kind of stupor, like some kind of drugged, sleep-walker. It is a waste of a life if one never wakes up from the dream and continues to cry over life's illusory difficulties. Staying on the treadmill of life is senseless and a little sad when all you have to do is shift your perspective and prioritise your values. For example, you attribute great importance to your achievements and are attached to recognition, awards, and accolades, which are all body-based worldly matters. You cannot take your trophies with you when you leave the body. You cannot take the memories of your accomplishments or all the praises you received. There will not be anyone applauding you after your body expires!

Why not use your competitive nature to find out who you are! Wake up! Shakeup! Wake up from this dream!

Death, loss and grief

When the time span of the body, say, of your husband, wife, closest partner or friend, comes to an end, you will tell others that you have lost your loved one. You will feel sad and start to grieve for your loss. But this, too, is an illusion! There is no such thing as death; therefore, where is the loss? Where is the place for grief? No one has died. This misunderstanding has arisen from perceiving ourselves and our loved ones as body-forms and identifying with all these forms.

You grieve because your loved one's body-form is no longer with you, and your world collapses! But this is a misunderstanding or wrong thinking. It is not Reality! In this imaginary world, your beloved has gone, but in Reality, he has not gone anywhere. He did not come, and he did not go; you did not come, and you will not go anywhere either! What has taken place is simply a transition. You have not lost anyone. Your beloved is not lost. His energy, what he is in essence has undergone a change, a transformation, transmutation from the form to the formless that we all are. The dissolution of the body does not affect our true nature. You are not the body, and neither are your loved ones. They live on!

We have always existed; we will ever exist. That is our Reality! But our fears of falling sick, of being alone, feeling unloved and afraid of dying and death, etc., keep driving us away from Reality, forcing us to keep on running. From what are we running? We are running from our imagined fears and losses. The concept of death follows us relentlessly, and so we keep running away from this ghost that keeps us in terror's grip.

Don't wait until the body is dying. Start attending to yourself now. Self-enquire, (see this Practice in Part 4: "Bootcamp"), and put an end to your illusory-based suffering! All your fears will leave you when you face them and discover that they are baseless. You will not have any more fear when you realize your true nature: you are not the body, but immortal.

Some people spend thousands of dollars investing precious time and energy, attending all sorts of therapy sessions and analyzing their intensely complex personalities, to help them cope better with their lives. And yet, it is all a passing show. If we all woke up, there would be no need for therapists. Why not awaken to Reality: your natural Stateless State, where there are no fears or hang-ups, just unwavering peace and unfluctuating happiness? Stop being a seeker! Be a finder, a finder of your authentic Self. That is the only way to be free. Chase the ghosts out of your head and set yourself free.

Part Two: Be All Ears!

"I came to this earth so that I could find my way back to the Beloved." Rumi

Chapter 7.
Find the Big Self!

"How do I find out who I am? I am reading books on personal growth. Will that help?" you may ask. There is nothing wrong with reading books on personal growth, self-improvement and personal development, nothing, except the goal: which is to improve and develop the "personal", when, in fact, the person is not the permanent "Big Self", the real self, the true self. These self-help books have flooded the market, along with many workshops on "emotional intelligence", "spiritual intelligence", "self-compassion", "self-motivation", the "law of attraction", "coaching", etc. The problem with all of these is that they address the illusory self and feed the ego, without exception. While helping you become a more all-round, efficient human being is a positive endeavour, the downside is that it reinforces your bodily identity and keeps the dream going.

The "Self-help" and "Self-improvement" market has always been popular, offering a variety of talks by motivational speakers, who tell you what your ego already knows - that "you are great!" These talks centre around the best self or the core self, encouraging you to be the "best version of you"! But is this self the true self? No one ever bothers to ask the question: "Which self are we talking about?" Invariably, there is the assumption that there is only the little self, the individual, based on the premise that we are all "separate selves": yourself, myself, herself, himself, etc.

Crippled inside

As long as we consider ourselves to be body-minds, there will always be a hunger for these books and expensive courses. Unfortunately, like food, they will only satisfy us for a brief moment, until we are hungry once more. (The goal here is to put everything aside - the questions, the searching, etc. We need to put all of this aside for good, which means the "seeker" and the "search".) If you take what is happening at face value, there will always be new dramas and problems.

These books may help you cope better with life, make you feel good about yourself, and even feel more self-fulfilled. That is very positive! You may even learn how to use one or two coping mechanisms: heal your wounds and patch yourself up temporarily using a band-aid to stop the haemorrhaging. Great! However, you will never be complete or whole if you identify with the body and take the world for real. All these books which address the mind and the emotions keep you firmly rooted in the dream! Because we do not know our true nature, we often see ourselves as weak, dependent and powerless human beings, in need of help and support from various quarters and different experts!

The popularity of these "Self-help" "Seminars" and "Intensives" has reached a peak, as they address a generation which - perhaps more than ever before – feels battered, bruised and broken under the pressures of life.

You are not a mind-body complex. You are that Spirit, that Presence, that expresses itself through the vehicle of the body. You have problems because you see yourself as an individual. When you alter your perception and see yourself as that powerful, untouchable Presence, your issues or obstacles may well still be around, but they will not affect you. When the illusory you, the imaginary self, dissolves, you will not need any self-improvement because there will be the realization that you are already perfect!

Who is reading?

Spiritual books and courses will not help you, if all they do is keep feeding you with more ideas and conceptual knowledge for you to get your head around. The only books that can, and will assist you, are those that demolish your misconceptions and misperceptions and push you inwards. All books contain second-hand knowledge. Reading spiritual books is harmless unless you read one after the other continuously, without ever reaching a conclusion. Hard as you may try, you will not be able to find the answer to your existence from books.

"You" cannot be found in books. It is vital, and even more pressing, that you investigate the "Reader". Find out who is reading? For whom are you reading? Get to know yourself! "Who am I?" The answer to this question can only come from within you. All the knowledge you have gathered to date is body-based; it is not your direct, empirical understanding. "She says this, he says that", what do you say? Search! Examine yourself! Examine everything that you know! Self-enquire, while you still can.

When, eventually, you wake up with the knowledge that you are not who you once thought you were, you will no longer be interested in bettering that illusory, small self. You will only be interested in Selfless Self, that one, formless omnipresent Universal Self that you are. Listen to the inner promptings of Selfless Self! Your Inner Master, is the only real Coach, Motivator, and Faithful Friend, that is with you for eternity.

When will you crack the code of your existence? When it finally dawns on you that you are not a separate self but part of a vast Oneness. And when this happens, you will tap into that eternal Source from which the nectar of all-consuming love flows. And like a fine wine, you will savour its bouquet and sip it slowly.

A golden opportunity

If you continue to operate with partial sight and ignore Reality, the disturbing notion of death will linger and pounce on you one day, filling you with fear and regret.

And then, with your life nearly over, you will exclaim, "Oh, what have I done, or not done! When I had the chance to be free, I ignored it. I let the shallow attractions of the imaginary world keep me enchained. My attachments kept me going round and round in circles, in that colourful but illusory carousel!" You missed a unique opportunity!

You want to stay within the circle of illusion because it is familiar and safe, and it keeps the predictable, and at best, entertaining show going. That is understandable, however, the real you is not some kind of robot built to act and react. Why not get out of the driver's seat and let Selfless Self drive you! Why not stop holding on tightly to everything, and instead, let Selfless Self direct you! You were never the doer, you just thought you were.

You are not the body or the mind but unborn and formless. You existed before beingness, and you will continue to exist after beingness. You are the central point of the universe. That is your Reality, the knowledge that was hidden from you.

So, how do we apply this knowledge to our daily lives? We do it with our dedication and self-involvement. We can usually only make progress when we throw ourselves wholeheartedly into a task. This transformation process is no different! When we are entirely involved in finding a solution to something, we find it because our concentration is complete and one-pointed. When you are absorbed in this knowledge and giving your undivided attention as you read, hear, practice and apply it, a transformation takes place. Soon you will see and feel some dramatic changes!

Better than winning the lottery

This knowledge will stop you in your tracks and make you pause. As it bypasses the mind, moving and stirring within you, you will experience a strong feeling of relief, something like: "Now, at last, I know! I know the secret of my existence. I have wasted so much of my time until now, but not anymore!" That feeling is indescribable, (better than any lottery win, which cannot ultimately change or relieve one's problems and depression). And later on, when you are older, you will have no regrets, none whatsoever.

Just drop it!

As you absorb the knowledge, you will learn to apply it to daily life. Here are four examples of how we "let the mind run away with us":

We have all heard ourselves saying, "It was one of those mornings" when things did not go the way we had planned. When this happens - instead of leaving the disruptions behind and continuing afresh - you carry the baggage of what went wrong and let it spoil the rest of the day. Before you know it, you are saying, "It was one of those days"! If something does not work out as you had expected, be alert, recognize it, and catch it quickly. Stop identifying with it! Just drop it!

The following example is about "self-talk": that familiar, negative voice in our heads that has the knack of catastrophizing everything. Say, you were expecting to go on holiday and had been excitedly counting the days. The holiday is suddenly cancelled! If you accept the cancellation, you can draw a line under it and move on. However, if you listen to the voice in your head, you will spend the next few hours or days, recounting and re-experiencing the numerous times throughout your life, when nothing went according to plan! And then you may move into self-pity mode, indulging yourself, reminding yourself that "nothing ever goes right for me!" Don't listen to that voice! You know it will always take you on a downward spiral. Stop identifying with the disappointment. Just drop it!

We have all experienced those instances when we did not feel appreciated. Say, you spend time and money choosing a special present for a friend, but she does not respond in the way you had hoped! She even tells you she doesn't like your gift. In this situation, don't get sucked into a long narrative, not only about no one ever appreciating what you do, but about no one ever appreciating you at all! Just drop it!

Finally, say you did not get an "A-grade" for one of your subjects. The record starts playing: "I'm a failure. I'm useless. I've always been useless. No one cares about me because everyone thinks I'm useless., too, etc.

They don't like me. I don't blame them because I don't like myself"...etc. Just drop it!

Throw all of these, and similar mental constructions in the trash! Carrying on in this way will keep you incarcerated in the dream. Don't follow the thought-patterns and feeling-patterns. If you apply the Practice to your daily life, you will get better and faster at spotting yourself falling into these habitual spirals. The stories you have identified yourself with are not true. They have nothing to do with you. They have been created by the ego. With regular practice, you will train yourself to disidentify from them, until you no longer identify with anything. Once you are free of the ego's trappings, life will unfold spontaneously.

When you wake up from this dream of life, you will no longer be in bondage. You will approach life light-heartedly and light-footed, gliding spontaneously, without letting anything touch, affect you, or bring you down.

Chapter 8.
Searching for Happiness

We are always searching for happiness and peace from outside sources because we remain oblivious of our real identity. We wander, travel, roam here and there. We try all sorts of things that will offer us lasting happiness and peace, as we attempt to fill that longing within us that is always seeking to connect, share and be part of a greater whole. Because we don't know who we are, we find ourselves continuously on the move, filling our lives with distractions, seldom able to remain still. We don't know that the destination is within, that we are the destination!

Some people even travel to Peru, Brazil, Costa Rica and other exotic destinations to experiment with mind-altering drugs at guided rituals. They do this hoping to "find themselves" or feeling trapped, they are looking for a way out to break free from their imaginary jails.

The dis-ease of isolation

We are always restless, looking for different forms of entertainment to help us escape from our deep sense of disconnectedness and isolation. We are looking for love to keep the discomfort and pain of our dis-ease at bay. However, we cannot find happiness and peace in the world. We will only find palliatives that offer a temporary fix.

We have collected so much baggage throughout our lives, and each day we accrue even more, never pausing to throw some of it out. How many of us take the time even once in a while, to look at ourselves, and find out where we are going, or from where we have come? Most of us don't know what we are doing half the time. We hope for the best, like throwing mud at the wall and hoping something will stick!

Endless diversions

We are obsessed with our body-image, spending much of our time, energy and money on our appearance, including cosmetic surgery - all of it to preserve our youthful looks. We continue to do this, despite knowing that we cannot reverse the ageing process. None of us can, including the beautiful people – the Brad Pitt's and the George Clooney's or the Naomi Campbell's, Kate Moss's, and suchlike. We need diversions all the time to de-stress us, bring us happiness and lift our spirit. The choices are endless!

When you stop looking for happiness from material sources and instead, look within, you will discover that you are the Source of happiness and peace. By then, you will no longer need to "lift your spirit" because you will have realized that you are that Spirit. That Spirit or Presence is Itself, in essence, spontaneous happiness and spontaneous peace. It does not age! It is forever pristine, untouched and unaffected.

"Demolition Course"

This book is not just another book of knowledge. Your Reality is beyond knowledge. The only information you will find here is how to go about destroying everything you think you know about yourself. You are on a demolition course that will excavate everything from you, that is not you. And for this, you need a metaphorical bulldozer! Let's take a look at the root of the problem!

As was mentioned earlier, a baby can be compared to a brand-new computer with mega storage space. It does not have any files on it, nor any memory. It is clean, empty, and devoid of history. Your Spirit is very sensitive. Long before you could talk, you were already absorbing everything you heard, and everything around you like a sponge.

Your illusory life began with listening, and gathering impressions that were recorded and saved onto your hard-drive. One by one, these impressions were fed into your beingness, stored in your big computer, and preserved for your imaginary future. For the vast majority of us, these early impressions will remain with us for a lifetime, influencing and shaping our lives, until we become aware of them.

You constructed your false identity using the concepts at your disposal which had been added, one by one, like building blocks. Everything you heard and sensed around you formed your self-perception, perception of the world, and apparent Reality. In time, and more or less, unconsciously, these concepts solidified and became the foundation stones of your existence and Reality.

Mental imprisonment

Years of listening to what you were told formed your personal identity. As you developed the personal self, your real identity was obscured, and eventually, buried and hidden from yourself. The sun always shines, even when the clouds hide it. Similarly, your Presence continued to shine, even though it was hidden under your make-believe world. Within the space of a few years, your authentic, untarnished identity was pushed out of view. Alienated from your true nature, your Spirit turned away from itself and was instead drawn to the attractions of the imaginary world, where your desires imprisoned you.

Put simply, the Spirit became attached to the body, to the seen, to the known. As life took its toll on you, you were trapped by these desires and even more disconnected from your Source. As this happened, your free, playful and spontaneous nature was crushed by society's rules and regulations that were imposed on you. You were suffocated by all those endless social norms, directives and orders which you had to obey!

When you identified with the body, you perceived your unlimited nature as limited. The One, omnipresent, unborn Self that you are was seen through the small eyes of a human being, who was by now, utterly convinced that she had taken birth, and was destined to die.

For many of us, the demands of work and home life deadened our Spirit and turned us into walking corpses. In this world of duality, these pressures weighed heavily on us. As it became increasingly difficult, consciously or unconsciously, for us to break free from this feeling of bondage, we settled for a grey existence - with fleeting moments of happiness, amid all the stresses and strains of life.

You don't have to settle for greyness. You don't have to be like the characters we have all heard stories about - full of regret and remorse, wondering what their lives were all about, or what went wrong! Let the sun shine again! Now you have a choice to uncover your true Self. How? By demolishing the original building blocks that formed your pseudo self.

The trap of body-based knowledge

The bottom line is that the wrong kind of knowledge conditioned you. Your education was made up of little more than programming, brainwashing, superimpositions and conformity. The more one was moulded by worldly knowledge, the more the ego or pseudo-identity grew. And as this knowledge fed the ego, the Heart, the core of your being, which not so long ago was open and inviting like a flower, began to close. Your childhood innocence, openness, trust, joy and happiness, etc., your carefree, intuitive nature, spontaneous understanding, and your Essence were all gradually suppressed and hidden.

Like it or not, you absorbed everything that you heard throughout your upbringing. Your parents alleged that you were born at a specific time, and therefore, your age was such and such. You were given a name and were told that your gender was either female or male, that you had, say, a "brother" or a "sister", or that you were an "only child". What followed was a whole series of labels attached to you, which apparently defined who you were. These very seeds that were planted in your early life, subsequently, grew into one almighty, gigantic tree.

Children are very sensitive to whatever they hear and experience. There are different kinds of abuse, physical, mental, emotional and sexual, where adults intentionally or unintentionally harm children. The abuse may take place over a long period, or it may be a one-off occurrence. Either way, these experiences leave a lasting and damaging impression. Many of them are traumatised and scarred for life. Neglect is also a form of abuse where a child, lacking in love, care, and attention, carries a sense of unworthiness and an entrenched feeling of being unlovable throughout life! E.g., some of you may have experienced psychological or emotional abuse from a dominant, overbearing parent, who told you that you were dumb or weak, useless, or even a "good for nothing"! These negative comments profoundly impact children, often staying with them as a voice in their heads for many years to come, if not, for the rest of their lives. All these impressions and experiences remain as sticky layers of the pseudo self which are difficult to remove because you have identified with them for so long.

Under pressure

The pseudo self, illusory ego or false "I", all the same, quickly formed into a "somebody", believing itself to be a separate entity with a unique, individual and often, competitive identity: "I am this. I am that". "I will make my mark in the world". Or, at the other end of the spectrum, "I am a failure, useless", or "I cannot cope". You saw others as competitors or even enemies. Every step of the way, the ego kept on growing, asserting itself, and falling under a spell of the many attractions the world seemed to offer. You did not know that you were the Source of everything, the Power, the Energy, the Light. Call it what you will!

As you took your place in the world, even though you hadn't a clue about who or what you were, you still had to cope with the many problems and difficulties that came your way, e.g., the demands from work, separation, divorce, single-parenting, physical illness or mental health issues, caring for a parent, grief, etc., etc. These difficulties caused you anxiety, worry and fearfulness.

Who am I? What is my true identity amidst all the struggle and strife? What motivates me? These are the questions to ask yourself. Find out! It is easy to see how we have blindly bought into this imaginary world. We have been bombarded from the very beginning by many influences, impressions, relentless demands and pressures from family, peers, society, etc. We have been brought up to compete, to do better than others, and to succeed in the world. We were all brought up with some knowledge that equipped us to function as individuals in the world. Since we are not individuals, and we are in the process of learning that the world is *Maya*, an appearance, we can now learn about our real identity. We can replace our misunderstanding with fundamental understanding.

The seeker

You lost your way early on in life when you started to listen. When the door to the imaginary world opened, you heard so many things that left their mark on you. Paradoxically, you noticed that the more you knew and the more you accumulated, the more you felt that something was missing. There always seemed to be a sense of lack, a hole that nothing could fill. You couldn't quite put your finger on it. Many times, you asked yourself the questions: "Who am I? From where did I come? What is the meaning of this life?" But you didn't find any answers. Maybe you picked up one or two books from time to time, and even visited a few teachers during your periods of searching, convinced that they knew more than you!

For some of you, this opened the door to "Satsang", which means "meeting in truth", where you could get together with fellow seekers for a couple of hours, in the hope of finding the answers you were seeking.

For others, Satsang just made you feel as if you were caught up in another loop, sometimes a costly one at that! None of the authentic Gurus of India etc. ever charged money for their teachings. They stated that money contaminated the Satsang – the mixture is incompatible. They would say: "Why pay for knowledge that is free? It is your innate knowledge for which there is no charge". When visitors to Shri Ramakant were getting ready to return home, they used to ask him if they could leave a donation. He always replied: "Yes! Before you go, deposit your mind, ego and intellect here. That is the best donation!"

In days of old, people would pray for direction, for guidance, for truth, but now, in our desperation to find happiness, we are prepared to pay for listening to half-truths and personalized versions of the truth.

Maybe you listened to various teachers, hoping they would have the answers to your questions, maybe even share with you the secret of their happiness. Perhaps you reached a dead end in your search and were left feeling even more disenchanted and confused. If you are still searching, convinced that there must be more to life, you are ripe and ready to absorb the teachings in this book,

Who Am I? This knowledge is your knowledge, universal knowledge, the missing Truth you have been longing to find!

Chapter 9.
Hammering

As was mentioned before, "right" and "wrong" are concepts, along with the rest of them. There is no right or wrong, but we need to use some terms to communicate. While you were growing up, you listened to a lot of worldly, body-based and deceptive information. But now you can listen afresh and hear the "right" kind of information. "Right knowledge" is the missing truth. Right knowledge is universal knowledge, your knowledge.

Your Spirit, that invisible Presence in you is sensitive and receptive. Listen to, and understand, the most profound knowledge of your Reality presented here!

Listen to your biography, your story - that is everyone's story. Be all ears! You have to hear it, not with the mind and the intellect, but with your whole being. Let it connect with your centre! Let it touch that place deep inside you that is full of longing. Your story is a true love story, the ultimate love story. Your fresh understanding and discrimination will empty out the illusory self.

Delete all the unwanted files from your computer - the accumulated beliefs, presuppositions, opinions, viewpoints, values, attachments, etc. When all of these have been removed, then, and only then, will Ultimate Reality emerge - that Thoughtless Reality that you are that is Self without self. When there is the realization that nothing exists apart from Selfless Self, you will have completed your "Demolition Course" and received your Master's degree: M.D. – Master of Demolition!

Beyond knowledge

You have embarked on the most incredible voyage of your life, the journey of self-discovery, so that you can find the answer to "Who am I?"

Why should you bother? What if you don't find the answer? What will you get? Why put yourself out? Because when you truly know yourself, you will leave behind the darkness of ignorance forever, and all your suffering will finally come to an end. What will be the result? The reward is causeless, permanent happiness and peace!

This knowledge is not aimed at the individual listener; it speaks to the invisible Listener in you, that invisible Presence, or Great Spirit, your Essence. This book is not a run of the mill book. Instead, it contains exceptional knowledge because it takes you beyond knowledge. It does not purport to offer you any new theories; in fact, it is not giving you anything new at all. It shows you what you have overlooked: "That" which is already within you, which is beyond time and space. It shows you your imperishable nature.

It is a challenging read because it asks you to forget about everything and discard and surrender all that is not you.

Repetition

If you find some of the text repetitive, that is both unavoidable and necessary. Reading, listening and hearing are potent tools. As you imbibe this knowledge over and over again, the mind loses its power. Accept what you are reading with Conviction, letting the words touch you. Listen to them, without analyzing them (as dissecting the terms in this way will only bring back the mind). Hammering home the same teachings, again and again, is essential so that all the beliefs, faith and confidence you have in the false notion of "I am somebody", are permanently crushed. Give up the primary, deeply ingrained concept that you are the body-mind complex. Identifying with this concept is the cause of all your troubles. It is the mosquito that keeps on biting you.

The spell of illusion you have been under is ignorance. Break the spell by understanding what you are. You were trained to act and react in specific ways, therefore, don't be surprised if you meet with some resistance as you begin to discard your mistaken identity. King Ego who has been sitting on your throne for so long, has no intention of abdicating. Like a jack in the box that keeps popping up, you must be ready to keep hammering him back down until it stays down for good. Be done with it! Press CTRL, ALT, DEL, and keep on hammering until you free yourself of all illusion.

Passing clouds - in and out of love

One of our biggest fantasies centres around "love". What do we mean by love? What is love, and who is loving whom, or what? The most popular songs are often those syrupy, cringe-worthy ones about feelings and emotions, relationships, falling in love, and falling out of love with someone. In other words, they are all about duality, the imaginary, and the transient. In Mariah Carey's haunting 1993 classic, *Without You*, (written by the rock band, "Badfinger" in 1970), she sings, "And now it's only fair that I should let you know what you should know/I can't live, if living is without you/ I can't live, I can't give anymore...".

Human love is partial, limited and imperfect love, if there is the delusion at play of an "I" who loves a "you" and an "I" who can give a "you" total happiness and make you complete. No one can make you whole or completely happy except yourself. Real and total satisfaction can only be found within you, as causeless happiness, which is part of your authentic nature. Relationships can teach us about ourselves, bring out our strengths and weaknesses, enrich and make us grow. They can make us feel whole. But the fact is we are already whole.

In healthy relationships, (which are not based on need - because two people recognize their own value and worth, and know where they stand), even in long-lasting, loving relationships where two people express the most profound love – this love is still a limited expression of that universal, unlimited love within all of us. It is a taste of a greater love that is unconditional and free from all attachments.

Songs about love and loss, happiness and sadness are odes to the dream! They are all expressions of this ephemeral, illusory dream that is the movie of our life! Every one of us wants to love and be loved, to be with someone, (sometimes anyone will do), so that we can enact a beautiful fairy tale, a love story that may lead to an engagement and marriage. But our dreams of living happily ever after often turn into nightmares because our love is ego-based and full of wants and needs for itself. Its agenda is one of getting, rather than giving. In these toxic relationships where self-worth is lacking, we tend to give value to our partners instead of ourselves. Therefore, it is not surprising that these relationships are bound to fail.

Brainwashed

The ego is the illusory "I", the false "I", the wrong "I". It is a layer covering your true Essence. Trace the source of the ego. From where did it come? When you investigate this "I", you will find out that it has no substance. You mistook the ego for yourself when you identified with the body-form: your name, sex, work, doership, etc. - all of which are the imagined layers on your Presence. Your true "I" is that nameless Reality that was, that is, and that will be always.

When the ego identified with the body-form, the survival instinct kicked in and you started protecting yourself. Your behaviour is a learned response, a chemical reaction to feeling vulnerable and fearful. As you grew fond of your bodily identity and started to accumulate more knowledge, more objects and more experiences from the world, as a direct consequence, you feared losing your possessions and attachments. Because of these influences, these superimpositions on Presence, you started to accept the BIG LIE and declared: "I am somebody! I am important", or, "I am no good" (same thing really). I am an individual. I this, I that, me, me, me... my this, my that, I want, I will have, etc.".

This feeling of separateness that is hard-wired in all beings and profoundly rooted, walks hand-in-hand, with the need for self-protection. The more you have, the more you have to lose, and the more you need to satisfy yourself. As a result of this primary misunderstanding of your true identity, the will to survive at all costs evolved and strengthened over a lifetime: "I am afraid." I don't want to die." "Help me!" etc.

Now we can unlearn and undo our learned behaviour! We were conditioned to guard our hearts and pockets, protect ourselves, and hide our vulnerability. But now, we can step aside and get out of our own way. Instead of shutting down, disconnecting and withdrawing, we can learn to walk with an open heart.

You are immutable

Your Reality is changeless. The mental or emotional climate may change, but you do not change. Sometimes you are happy, and at other times, you feel sad or anxious. Sometimes you are calm and peaceful, and at other times you experience depression. Everything comes and goes, except you. You are always the same! The thoughts may be constant, but they need not disturb you. Just be! The seasons come and go, but you are not going anywhere. You are immutable.

Functioning as a person takes a lot of energy, but you are not a person or a somebody. You are formless and unborn! Now is the time to come out of your whole, illusory existence! Slow down the "doing" and start being a human being, not a human doing! There is no birth and there is no death. You have nothing to fear. You are immortal, perfect, and free. There is only one obstacle that stands in your way of finding out who you are, and that is for you to carry on thinking that you are somebody, when in fact, you are nobody – no body, no-thing! You have lived your life under the illusion of being a person and have accumulated many layers of illusion as a consequence. When you peel off these skins one by one like peeling an onion, you will eventually wake up and see that it was all a mirage! When you realize what you are, and live like that, you won't need any energy to function, as you will be in your natural Stateless State.

Listen up!

Look at yourself! Examine yourself! Concentrate on yourself! This is the way to root out all the impressions and influences (that have stuck to you, and are with you), so that you can be transformed back to your Original, Stateless State of "I am the Absolute". Here you are listening to your Truth, your Reality, over and over again.

When you hear your Truth, it has the effect of stirring and reawakening your Reality. That Reality has always been there, though buried deep. Reading, listening and hearing your Truth plugs you into the Source and resurrects your innate happiness, peace and love. As the knowledge of this Principle (You are Ultimate Reality), your Principle, your Reality, is hammered home, slowly and gradually, you will begin to live as That. You are already That, but you don't know that you are. However, when you repeatedly hear the same thing, inevitably, you will come to believe and accept it.

This knowledge, in tandem with Self-enquiry and Meditation, (as well as other recommended Practices in Part 4), will result in the "Spontaneous Conviction" of your true nature. (This Conviction is Self-Realization, which means that the illusory ego, the false "I", pseudo-self, or whatever was obscuring our Supreme Self, has dissolved. This Stateless State is your true, essential nature, permanently established.)

For the Spontaneous Conviction to arise, you need to unlearn everything you have learned via your upbringing and environment. That includes concepts such as "good", "bad", "happiness", "sadness", "tradition", "culture", "conduct", "merit", "sin", "guilt", "values", "karma", "rebirth", and for some, "heaven", "hell", and all the rest of the junk that you were spoon-fed. This knowledge that was planted in you, and absorbed by you, has to be thrown out, ejected and dissolved because it has nothing to do with who, or what, you are. Wearing the mask of being a person who is carrying heavy burdens, is way too costly. There is always a high price to pay, when sooner or later, the pressure cooker explodes, as the strain of it all finds an outlet in the manifestation of physical, emotional or mental problems.

The Universal condition - chronic illusion

We so-called human beings, are first and foremost Spirit beings, not just physical beings. We are suffering from chronic illusion which makes it difficult, almost impossible, to see ourselves in any other way than as finite beings.

The only cure for this malaise is a change in perspective. The dis-ease must be rooted out at the source. Backtrack to your childhood before all the illusory add-ons covered over your identity. Challenge every one of your deep-rooted values and attachments.

Examine your stance, everything you hold dear, intellectual, personal, emotional, economic, social, familial, ethical, political, experiential, spiritual, anything with an "ism" or "ology" behind it, etc., etc.

Look at all the knowledge you have accumulated to date, all that you think you know: the book learning and theories, including the philosophies you may have adopted, religious traditions, etc. From where did all of this knowledge come? Does it belong to you? Is it part of your inherent, innate nature, or only part of your conditioning? Bring everything under the microscope and take a good look at your belief systems. Do they belong to you? Challenge the validity of all these ideas, preconceptions, and everything you have learned from as far back as you can remember.

As you absorb the knowledge and find out for yourself, what is true and what is false using the practice of Self-enquiry, you will discover that all you know in totality is "body-based knowledge", "body-related knowledge", "second-hand", etc., accumulated from the world. Prior to beingness, there was no "body" and no "knowledge". Therefore, everything to date, all the knowledge you have amassed, is second-hand knowledge, time-bound, and sourced from the outside. In other words, it is not who you are, nor anyone else. Clean the slate!

Chapter 10.
Stand Naked

Remove all the superimposed layers, your whole illusory disguise, including the concepts, memories, experiences, etc., until you stand naked! Forgetting everything is the name of the game! Forget yourself to find your Self!

Who am I? Get to know the real you by eradicating everything that does not belong to your nature. Dropping all the worldly add-ons is the only cure for this sickness. At present, you know yourself only in the body-form with its chattering mind, proud intellect, puffed up ego, or ashamed, with a deflated ego - either way, it is the same, all still about the "little me" with never-ending needs. You are not that!

Loosen and remove all your attachments to concepts, ideologies, beliefs, etc., basically, to thought in general. You need to be ruthless and scrutinize everything perceivable and conceivable. One by one, your concepts will evaporate. Dissect and investigate everything you consider to be the "norm" or its opposite – they are all concepts. This process will explode the myth of your bodily identity, sense of self and perception of the world. It will destroy the very constructs of your Reality and self-image.

Burst the hot air balloon that carried you adrift throughout this long dream of life. Shoot down all the goals, and wake up! Make waking up your primary goal! The only way you can do this is by cutting through the thick and sticky layers of the imagined you. Excavate deeper and deeper with Self-Enquiry, meditation and mantra recitation (see Part 4) until you have rooted out your attachments to the entire infection.

Shaking the foundations

Shake your fragile foundations and demolish your comfortable house. In time, the foundations you built with the "I am the body" identity, will start to crumble. This whole process of breaking down to break through is necessary to pave the way for Reality to establish itself on rock solid foundations.

Eventually, you will come to know that the body is a material body, and everything this material body knows is material knowledge. To reawaken Reality in you, to be that Reality, and find your Knowledge from within, all you need to do is erase everything, using the Practice Tools (see Part Four: "Bootcamp"). Self-Knowledge is Real-Knowledge. It is knowing yourself as Reality, after waking up from the dream.

Using a process of elimination, you will be able to discover for yourself what you are not. After you have done that, then That which you are will emerge: Ultimate Reality. Put this knowledge into practice and watch your affliction gradually heal itself, until it is completely eradicated from your system. When you have peeled away all the layers, you will arrive at the Source. And when you plug into your Source, it will herald the beginning of a wondrous unfolding, filling your life with causeless, abundant happiness.

Bliss amphetamine

Some of you have been drowning in ignorance and sadly intoxicated by the aches and pains of your mortality. After drinking in this knowledge, you will be intoxicated with immortality - the nectar of bliss! A mystery awaits. Magical energy is already inside you, waiting to be discovered, like a true lover or soul-mate eagerly and impatiently wishing to share all his secrets with you. It is like embarking on an ecstatic trip, without taking any MDMA! It is like taking a bliss amphetamine, without the need for a tranquillizer afterwards, as there is no comedown.

When you apply this knowledge and practice to your daily life, Reality will be revealed - Ultimate Truth, Ultimate Reality. You are That! When the dream is over and the bubble finally bursts, you will know first-hand that you are unborn. That Spontaneous Conviction will arise. You hold the key to the highway - the highway to freedom, liberation!

Wrong default settings

There was an error in your computer when it was set to the wrong default settings. This mistake pushed you in the direction of accepting the body-mind complex as your Reality. As your friendship with the body-form grew, you became firmly attached to the idea of satisfying your bodily needs, like preening yourself in front of the mirror maybe too many times a day, constant retail therapy, obsessive dating, sex, or treating yourself just a little too often, to comfort food.

Your attachments kept you small, weak, and at times, fearful, even powerless. Get yourself out of this entangled web of illusion! As long as you keep identifying with the body-mind, loving it excessively, your problems will continue to cause you grief. As long as there is love and affection for, and attachment to, the temporary, the non-permanent, you will not be able to find real, lasting peace. You will just gravitate from one problem to the next. Be courageous! It takes guts to leave behind the familiar and let go of everything you know.

Shed your old skin

You may have a fierce resistance to letting it all go. Maybe you are reluctant to give up your lifestyle along with all the knowledge you have gathered to date: your ideas, concepts, beliefs, philosophical, metaphysical, religious, spiritual or scientific concepts that you adopted from numerous books and many other sources. The choice is yours! Hang onto your self-image, staying as you are, small, safe and imprisoned, or say "Yes" to experiencing yourself as an infinite being!

Leave behind this illusory world! Self-investigate and find out, "Who am I?" Why this life?" What is the definition of "good"? What is the meaning of "bad"?" Good luck or bad luck! Such values belong to the circle of duality. The love you have for your pseudo-identity is a habit that just kept on growing! You made a religion out of it because you did not know any better. Gradually, however, when you discover for yourself that you are not who you thought you were, you will be released from that intense and imprisoning grip. And thankfully, after this colossal shake-up, you will fly out of the cage as a sage, breathe and really be able to live. When you realize your true nature, you will not be disturbed or rattled by anything. The difficulties and problems will continue, but they will not affect you. You will not behave in the way you used to act, whether short-tempered, angry or reactionary. The continuous shedding of your old skin will ultimately reveal your divine light.

Be firm and patient

Throughout your life, you have given the mind, the ego, and the intellect great value and importance. These illegal tenants have been living in your house for so long, that it is not surprising they are resistant to change and unwilling to leave. You can't expect them to vacate the premises without your putting in some effort.

Transformation takes time. Let your Inner Listener listen and absorb everything. That Divine Essence that you are does not have any experience of being an individual. The real you that is your Essence has never been touched, tainted or changed in any way, by pain and suffering, happiness or unhappiness, or any other pair of opposites. You are immutable; you have always been immutable. You are the same always. Let this knowledge penetrate! There is no difference between you and everyone else, except for the body-form. Presence is one; Source is one. Presence is shapeless. There is only one Essence. There are no friends or enemies in Oneness! Boyfriends, girlfriends, partners, wives, husbands, the pain experienced from relationship break-ups, the broken hearts – all of these are part of the mirage, the passing show, the transient and unreal appearances which often resemble a blockbuster movie!

Chapter 11.
Learning to Dance Again

Listen to your story! Your story is universal. The real you is infinite, forever free, bliss itself. When you listen to this Knowledge, the Truth of your existence, there is a feeling of complete peace. This re-cognition and fundamental understanding makes you forget about yourself and your false identity. Your Spirit, your sensitive Inner Listener is slowly awakening. It is beginning to move, sway; it is learning to dance again.

Your Inner Listener is listening. Quietly and calmly, it is absorbing everything. Perhaps you are not aware, maybe you don't understand some things, but your Inner Listener accepts everything because there is resonance. Meditate on this knowledge! When you are quietly happy just being with this knowledge, you are experiencing true meditation that is natural and effortless.

After hearing this Knowledge and dwelling on it, churning it over and over, meditating and contemplating on Reality, there will be a breakthrough, something like: "At last! I have found what was missing all along. Now I know what I have been searching for and struggling to find. Got it! Finally, everything has fallen into place".

The dream world is made up of our desires for possessions, wealth, property, fame, etc. We want family and friends, sensual happiness, money, status and reputation etc. All these desires kept us in the dream world. While we were playing with fake, worldly wealth, we had forgotten about our natural, inner, sacred wealth.

Listen to these teachings with total concentration. Let them resonate! It is your innate Knowledge that is revealing itself to you! This is your biography, the story of your true identity. Listen and hear with attentive care!

Alchemy

This knowledge has the power to transform, like the alchemist who turns base metal into gold. For some of you, it may feel like aeons since you embarked on your search for wholeness and a return to the Source. That Source is deep in your heart. You are that Source.

Your Reality is not dependent on faith. It is not a question of needing faith; faith does not enter the equation. With or without faith, Reality is Reality, and you are That! (Initially, you may need to trust the knowledge presented here to give yourself the best chance for that shift in perspective to take place!) This knowledge has the power to reawaken and reignite your inner spark, that Light that was dimmed for such a long time. You are the Source of happiness and peace. Where you stand is the Ultimate!

When the ego-mind stops resisting, you will realize that you have finally found the link in the chain you had always felt was missing. That gnawing and sometimes painful feeling of alienation and lack will finally disappear.

There are no separate selves. There is no difference between any of us. That which speaks and listens is one and the same Essence. I am you, and you are me, sharing one Reality. When you know what you are not and have hammered the illusory you to death using the practices of Self-Enquiry, discrimination, meditation, etc., you will no longer have any concepts left.

You are the witness of the dream

Use your discrimination! Think about what is real and what is unreal by sifting through all that is impermanent and disidentifying yourself from these. Witness this long dream of life! Don't waste each day caught up or utterly lost in the dream! This is today's dream, and tomorrow's will be different. Don't give so much attention to the dramas.

Sometimes when we go to the movies and watch a great film, we don't want it to end because it is so good and entertaining. Similarly, we have been enjoying, or suffering, the movie of this life to excess, when it is, in fact, illusory, like the images on the screen. As long as we keep living as something or someone other than our true nature, this purest and highest knowledge will just remain words, and sadly, go to waste.

The body-form that you hold is the medium through which you can find happiness. You will miss out on authentic, permanent happiness if you continue to look for fleeting moments of material happiness from the material world.

"You" were missing

You are already whole and complete. Nothing is missing! You felt lost, but you were never lost; your Essence was simply obscured. Your Presence is, was, and will be always. Now you are being shown the map. If you read it carefully, it will take you Home.

You were baptized into a vast pool of fake news (all worldly news is fake) that diverted you off-course. All worldly knowledge comes from ignorance passed on from one generation to another. We were all subjected to the same treatment!

When you ask, "Who am I?", you will discover all the things that you are not, namely, the body, the thoughts and feelings, perceptions, etc. Be determined! Keep erasing everything until there is nothing left. Keep at it until the bubble bursts!

All your desires, hopes, ambitions and goals come from the false identity which you started accepting in childhood. Life's highest goal is to know yourself. For that to take place, you need to demolish all the fake bricks that were used to construct your illusory dwelling house. Ultimate Reality will not reveal itself until this happens.

Chapter 12.
Don't Live and Die as a Mere Mortal!

How can it be possible for us not to get caught up in life's dream, when it just seems to sweep us along at speed? We need to learn how to start pressing the pause button. How can we do this when we seem unable to meet all the demands of our working life and home life? We need to slow down the engine! Remind yourself that you are not the doer! Everything will not fall apart if you pause. Take some power naps and alone-time. Train yourself to be, to just be, without doing anything. Train yourself to enjoy your very own space. If you do not awaken to your true nature, it means you will live and die as a mere woman or man – pretty much asleep from the womb to the tomb.

Easy and difficult

So, how easy is it to find out who you are? It is both easy and difficult. If you are eager and earnest, it is easy. If you have a burning desire to find out what your existence is all about, this drive alone will motivate and propel you forward. What makes it difficult is that in order to inherit the treasure, you must reject everything you have accepted as valid until now. There is no doubt you need some courage to let go of everything you mistakenly thought was you!

We are attached to so many things. It is no wonder we still find it challenging to give them up, even when we know they are false. Here, when we say "give up", we are talking about a shift in perception, a change of view, internal detachment, mental detachment, emotional detachment. Self-surrender or renouncement does not mean physically abandoning or separating yourself from your family, friends or things. Not at all! It means using discernment and discrimination to disidentify and detach from, these powerful and controlling forces and attachments. Understanding dissolves ignorance. We are using a thorn to remove another thorn. Both thorns are illusory; nevertheless, when the "right" knowledge takes the place of "wrong" knowledge, the illusion dissolves. Put very simply, when you supplant the concept of "I am a woman" or "I am a man" with "I am Ultimate Reality", the light of awareness shines.

Dynamite

You have tremendous power which was concealed and hidden from you. It remained hidden from you because you kept looking out instead of in, and this gave you absolute faith and confidence in your body-based life. By listening to this knowledge of your Ultimate Reality, your Ultimate Truth, your innate power will gradually reveal itself. This knowledge is dynamite that will effectively smash, blow up, and shatter all your experiences to pieces. It will wipe the floor of your worldly wisdom, explode your comfortable house, and shake your crumbling foundations until your Reality is unearthed. When this happens, you will realize that you are completely separate from this world. And then, the Spontaneous Conviction that you are prior to everything will arise.

Treasure chest

Use this fantastic opportunity to know first-hand, the answer to the fundamental question of your existence, "Who am I?" Your invisible Presence is the Source, the only Source. You are not the body, but its sustainer. Everything is within you. Self-discover! Delve deep within and find your gold, the treasure that will give you permanent freedom! Your search will come to an end when you realize that you are everything and everything is in you. And when you open the treasure chest, slowly, slowly, you will find total fulfilment.

Who is suffering?

When non-duality replaces duality, it drives away the concepts of pleasure and pain, good and bad, right and wrong, suffering, and especially our fears surrounding death. There is so much misery, dissatisfaction and lack of peace because we are looking for answers in the wrong places. We are looking for the real in the unreal. We do not know that we are what we are seeking! We do not know that all the answers to our questions can only be found within us. Sometimes you may feel anxious or sad, depressed, in pain, and suffering. At other times, you may feel happy, peaceful, relaxed, yet at the same time, a little on edge because you know that these feelings are temporary and will soon pass. Who is anxious? Who is depressed? Who is happy? Who is suffering? Find out!

An end to suffering

Happiness and peace in abundance are yours for the taking. When these teachings and practices take hold, there will not be any more tension, anxiety or fear. When you no longer identify with the body-form, your disturbances and worries will lose their significance and begin to fade. When you stop thinking of yourself as a mere woman or man, you will have the strength and courage to face any challenges that come your way. How come? Because you will know deep down, without a shadow of a doubt, that whatever happens, happens to the illusory body, and not to you. When you know yourself with Conviction, nothing can ever affect or upset you again. That former "pseudo you" has gone! When you stop identifying with the body-form, you stop suffering. The real you cannot suffer!

Chapter 13.
Awakening

Who is awakening? Nobody! What is awakening? That something inside you that you thought was missing is stirring and awakening from its slumber. Read this knowledge as your biography. It is the story of the one Presence, one Spirit; it is the story of your eternal life. If you read it in this way, you will not find any separation or duality between the reader and the knowledge. You are one with the Knowledge that is your Reality. This knowledge is not just about understanding the mystery of your existence. It takes you beyond knowledge, beyond the mind, beyond understanding. When you understand something, that something is separate from you, try to apprehend what you are, instead of comprehend! You are the Reality.

Refreshing clarity

As you are reading this, the memory of your identity is refreshed and prompting you to awaken from the trance. That unseen Presence in you is pulled in, attracted by the words and vibrations and drawn to listen to its own story! That something inside you that you thought was missing is slowly awakening from its coma.

You don't have to believe in this knowledge. The absorption of it alone tells you it is Truth. It is not known intellectually, but intuitively, with apperception. You know it is your truth. Like sleeping beauty awakened by a kiss, the kiss of truth is felt from the inside.

Aha! Moment

When all your body-based knowledge has dissolved, and the Self-effulgent light shines, you will experience beautiful breath-taking moments of happiness and peace. The process of awakening will make you realize more and more that this insufferable existence is just a dream! The sheer joy and freedom of these "aha" moments often release tremendous, uncontrollable laughter. With clear seeing, you will suddenly KNOW: "I was not all of this after all... all my trials and tribulations were make-believe"... etc.

With these bursts of awakenings, it will suddenly dawn on you that the mind was just making up stories all the time. As you begin to witness things from a detached position, you will see everything differently. And as you continue to absorb the knowledge more deeply, your understanding will grow sharp and subtle. It will take a little time to progress from this stage of awakening – these light bulb moments of enlightenment – to reaching full "Self-Realization", where finally, that Supreme Reality is established.

Expect the occasional regression on the way. And don't be too hard on yourself when it happens. How long did it take to build your imaginary life with all its attachments? It did not happen overnight. So, be kind to yourself, and above all, be patient.

Your eternal right to your eternal knowledge

When Reality is accepted, there is liberation. The benefits of realizing yourself as Ultimate Reality are immeasurable, priceless! You will never be sad, unhappy, depressed, fearful, stressed, disturbed or lonely again. You will not have any questions! Every question that has ever arisen about your existence emerged from a body-form perspective. The questions appeared because you were searching for your natural home using the mind, while still blind to your true identity beyond the mind. Reality silences the noisy mind!

Everyone can experience Reality. It is not difficult, as long as you are willing to listen, contemplate and absorb. Digest all that has been conveyed here. Feast on it! It is food for the unborn. Bliss food that transforms the beggar into a millionaire! When you have tasted freedom, you will not be able to stop yourself from wanting more and more.

Everything is within you. You already have the whole package. This knowledge is a shining light that illuminates and shows you that same light in you. When you replace wrong knowledge with right knowledge, the former is removed 100%. The result of this process is the direct knowledge of your unborn state. Finally, you know who you are

See the invisible!

Apply yourself and be earnest! All that is needed is your involvement, motivation, impetus, and fiery determination. You were searching for the answers outside. How come you did not find them? Because the Finder is you! You are the Finder.

You are a Master in sole charge of your life. There is no other Master but you. You are a powerhouse, the only powerhouse and Source of energy. There is no point looking for power elsewhere in the world, as the world is your projection, your reflection. Everything starts and ends with you. Enlarge your vision, tap into your immense Power and "see" the invisible! Your invisible identity is your target.

Wake up from the stupor!

When you discover the truth of your nature wholeheartedly, it will move you, shake you out of your stupor, and profoundly awaken you. This Truth is your indisputable, immovable Truth. The body and all that you take yourself to be is not your identity. Your Presence is everywhere like the sky. Wherever you are, your Presence is there. These are the facts. The mystery or secret of your existence is unravelling. Who am I? There is no "Who?" What am I? There is no "What?" You are beyond words! At last, everything is becoming clear!

Don't read this book to dissect the words and analyze their meanings. Don't read it to take part in stimulating discussions on philosophy, metaphysics, spirituality, etc.

You are reading and absorbing this knowledge to forget about your bodily identity and cure you of your amnesia, so that you can recover the memory of your long-forgotten identity.

Part Three: I Am Unborn

"The lover visible, the Beloved invisible: whose crazy idea was this?" Rumi

Chapter 14.
You Are Before Everything

You have always existed and you will ever exist because you are unborn! You are prior to the world, prior to beingness, prior to everything.

Prior to beingness, you did not have any desires. There was no need for food. You did not go to "Burger King" or "McDonald's" for your usual double cheeseburger and fries. There was no need for entertainment using Twitter or Facebook. There was no material wealth or sensual pleasures. There were no holidays; you weren't drinking tequila sunrise on the beach! There were no iPhones or X-boxes. You did not have to take a shower, soak in a bubble bath, or even brush your teeth.

Prior to beingness, you did not have any relations or friends. There was no such thing as a "family life". You did not have any associations or interactions with others because there were no "others". What was your existence like before this dream began? All the different kinds of emotions, such as joy, sadness, excitement, peace, etc., did not exist before beingness. You are not connected to any of these. There were no such things as happiness or unhappiness, boredom or depression, fear, stress, suffering, vulnerability and insecurity.

These words and experiences appeared afterwards, in the world of duality. You acquired language for the body-form and accumulated knowledge for the body-form. Prior to beingness, there were no words and meanings, such as "affection" and "love". Nothing conceivable or perceivable existed. No-thing!

The menu is not the meal

Language belongs to the world of duality. All the words, concepts and terms we use today are responsible for complicating our search for Truth and creating a great deal of confusion. Your Reality has nothing to do with words. We created all the words and their meanings, such as "awareness", "consciousness", "I am", etc. These words are indicators or pointers; they are not the real deal – just like the menu is not the meal! You are Reality; there is only one Reality. We are all part of that same, one Reality. The name or label you ascribe to your Reality does not matter. We make the same mistake time and again, convinced that if we can name our essential nature, our Reality, then we have "got it"! You cannot pin down Reality; you cannot catch hold of it. What is conveyed here is beyond words. Don't mistake the terms for the Reality! Place yourself before beingness, wordless and silent!

You existed before the body-form and you will continue to exist after the body-form expires. Prior to beingness and after beingness, point to your Reality. That formless Reality is a non-dual Reality, a thoughtless state, without a knower, knowledge, experiencer, or any experiences. There is only "One Silent Essence, Unity, Oneness"! It is a placeless place, a Stateless State, empty of everything, both conceivable and perceivable! In other words, you cannot imagine it! In that abode, language is redundant, as there is no need for communication.

You are eternal

You know you exist. You don't need any proof to know this because your existence is self-evident. And what about your existence before manifesting as the body-form? Some of you may say: "I haven't a clue", "I don't know!" or "I did not exist!" But many of us feel a certainty deep in our very core. There is something inside us, a feeling, a knowing of our prior existence and eternal nature.

You may sense that you existed before manifesting as a body-form while at the same time, you don't know how, or in what way. But you know! That something, that knowingness, that Spirit or Presence, or whatever you may wish to call it, is the sacred flame that burns eternally. That invisible, unidentified identity is your eternal Source.

Prior to the mind

Who am I? The mind cannot answer this question because you are prior to the mind, prior to the ego, prior to the intellect.

From that formless, stateless, thoughtless, unknown existence, there emerged a body-form and consciousness. Consequently, when you became aware you existed, you reached a false understanding: "I am a body, an individual with a mind, an ego and an intellect". When this misunderstanding happened, you began to feed off worldly information. Taking up your position as a form, a somebody, a state, caused you all sorts of problems, difficulties and confusion. Fake news says: "I am a body-form that was born and, therefore, will die". Reality says: "I am formless, unborn, and, therefore, immortal".

We have all had some sort of inkling that there is much more to us than this body-mind. We are not just mere, mortal human beings, though we sometimes don't behave much better than the animals - living our lives, as if we are these gross bodies. We forget that we are walking temples, as it is only through the vehicle of the human form that Self-Realization is possible. In Reality, we are formless, unborn. We do not have a beginning or an end. Our origin is prior to beingness.

A mystery unto yourself

Your Presence existed prior to the world. When amnesia descended, you forgot about your true identity. Forgetting meant that your true nature remained a mystery unto yourself.

When your Presence or Spirit came together spontaneously along with the elemental body, duality began. When you started to know yourself as the body-mind, and identified with that, the reign of "King Ego" also began! You bought into the dream, accepted all the thought-forms, etc., without any discrimination, and really believed that you were somebody. In Reality, you are nobody – no-body. The body is not your identity. It is your spontaneous appearance, your reflection. Put simply, when you look at yourself in the mirror you see a reflection which is not you. You see your physical body, which is not what you are. How can your eyes see you when you are the Source of sight? You are hidden inside, under the covering of your body.

Having assumed your false identity as a woman or man, you deluded yourself into believing you were the initiator of all things, the "action woman" or "action man", the doer who was in charge of doing and controlling everything. That is where you went wrong. You gave away your power to the ego, believed in the ego's power, and bowed to its majesty. You became subservient to King Ego, following his dictates and serving his needs.

Chapter 15.
You Are Not the Doer

American Brian Rose, based in the U.K and host of a popular talk show that "introduces fascinating people in the world, from all walks of life", is one example of someone who was convinced he was the doer of actions. Climbing the career ladder almost destroyed him. Once a successful banker, he developed a drug and alcohol dependency, eventually collapsing under all the pressure. Flying high nearly killed him! Like so many others, however, he is one of the lucky ones. After reaching his nadir and hating his life, his work and himself, he succeeded in turning his life around.

Spontaneous existence

You may have thought you were in charge and made everything happen, but you now know that was only ego talk. You are not the doer. Your existence is spontaneous. There is no "you" who is doing anything. Contrary to what we may have believed, everything happens spontaneously. Perceiving yourself as the body-form and taking everything for real was the cause of the confusion. Leave behind this misperception! Your Spontaneous Presence is behind everything. Without the Power of Presence, you cannot "do" anything. You are not even capable of thinking.

"I'm not the body. I'm not the mind. I'm not the ego or the intellect. I'm unborn". Let this understanding be your Reality! When the knowledge of your true nature penetrates and breaks down the illusion of who you once thought you were, when everything liquidates, you will come to know for yourself that the entire world is your spontaneous projection: "I used to think I was in the world, but now, I know the world is within me." That will be your realization.

Give up your old habits of assessing and evaluating everything using the mind and the intellect. Don't let King Ego control you any longer, by keeping you in a constant state of busyness and stress – which he loves to do – watching you do this or do that, so that you never have any space left to just be! Don't get lost in the business of doing. Instead, allocate more and more time to being. Let the transformation take place! Contemplate on your Presence! Don't give any head space to personal worries, anxieties and problems. Be in that impersonal space!

When all the illusion has dissolved at the final stage and you no longer identify with the body, you will be gifted with a priceless and indescribable reward: unimaginable, blissful contentment! You are already Reality with all these riches, but you have not seen this for yourself. You have not taken the time out to look deep within, to know and experience what you are. Find out what you are! Your ultimate purpose is to wake up from this dream-life.

We were misguided into thinking and believing in "doership". This misunderstanding caused us endless problems, with many of us thinking that we were invincible, burning the candle at both ends - resulting in burn-out, addiction and death. We have seen many celebrities turning to alcohol or drugs to solve their problems as they battled with emotional and mental health issues. It has happened to so many, including Mariah Carey and Ben Affleck. Sadly, talented musicians such as Avicci and Amy Winehouse didn't make it. At the same time, other celebrities managed to turn the corner, such as Aerosmith's Steve Tyler, who for now, has managed to halt the downward spiral and sobered up. As these celebrities emerged from their dependency on drugs or alcohol, they still faced another challenge, namely, "What is going to replace the drugs, alcohol, prestige and money?"

We are all addicts

Russell Brand, comedian, actor, author and activist, is another celebrity who has been to hell and back. He is now using his experiences constructively: earnestly helping many people through his books, talks and self-help programme.

"This is the age of addiction", says Russell. "We are all addicted to something because we are off-centre, unhappy and alienated." How true! We will never find complete happiness and peace as long as we consider ourselves to be mere body-minds, who take everything for real.

Don't buy into whatever is happening around you. The combination of Presence and the five elemental body created our dream world. Identifying ourselves as separate individuals who are disconnected from everyone else, has dramatically complicated our dream existence, which we call "our perfect, or not so perfect, life".

The Dream

Before beingness there was nothing: no world, no other, no relationships or family life, no interactions and associations whatsoever. This whole dream began when Presence fused spontaneously with the body.

You can compare this life to dreaming. When you dream, you see many different landscapes. Say you dreamt about being on vacation, enjoying a holiday by the ocean, in glorious sunshine, with your family and friends. All of a sudden, on waking up, that whole dream world vanishes. Where did it all go? What happened to your family and friends, the ocean, the sun? You don't know, and you are not interested because you know it was a dream! When you are dreaming, you are the sole actor projecting all these different images. Likewise, your life is a series of dreams projected by you. This life is one long dream! Before the body, you were formless; after the body expires, you will remain formless. When the body dissolves, are you going to ask, "What happened to my family and friends? Where did the world go?

See the waking life as an extended version of your dream life! When we wake up from our dreams, we don't tend to dwell on them. We ignore them, or if they were unpleasant, we are very relieved when we wake up! When you know you are dreaming, you don't take your behaviour or actions in the dream seriously. Similarly, you will stop taking everything so seriously when you see this life as a long dream. The ego is absent in deep sleep. It is not there to say, "I did this", or "I did that". As you continue to rid yourself of the misconceptions and awaken from the dream, you will be able to live life without the ego – light and free, instead of heavily burdened.

Worldly identity

All our thinking processes are related to our body-based, accumulated knowledge, worldly identity, and our status in society, e.g., "I'm a psychologist", "I am a builder". "I am a mechanic". "I am a doctor, manager, travel agent, lawyer, etc.". "I am a mother", or "I am a father". I'm a spiritual woman or man. Were you any of these things prior to beingness? And will you be any of these things after the body disappears? You are none of these things. These are only the roles you have taken on and play out in the dream world.

All your worldly relationships, attractions and influences, including your material gains, hanging onto your fortune and building your empire, etc., all of these gave you temporary happiness, some relief from the stresses of life, and maybe one or two "highs". From experience, these highs were quickly followed by "lows", when you found yourself needing something more to alleviate the boredom and lift your spirit. But now that you are aware you were caught up in a never-ending cycle on the treadmill of life, you can finally stop running. Loosen all the attachments to your impermanent, worldly identity. Identify the permanent!

Attachment to your dream family

And what about your family attachments? What will happen to your family after you leave the body? All your relations are body-based: mother, father, sister, brother, friend. The entire world is your spontaneous reflection, including your dear family.

We have great affection for the body and its body-formed relations such as our families. They are also part of the grand illusion! The family did not exist before the body-form; it will not exist after the body-form expires. That said, you have a responsibility to take care of your family.

Recognize the family as part of the dream, the unreal drama. Everything, the world and society, including all your family members, are appearances in the dream. That said, your family is not a hurdle to Self-realization.

Just begin to slightly loosen your attachments to them and everyone else, so that you can see everything, without exception, as a dream. When you know life is a dream, your problems will not affect you. Being "in the world, but not of the world" means you are acting in a dream, knowing at the same time, that you are separate from it.

Suppose you have a problem that causes you pain and suffering. It happens because you believe you are a separate person and identify with the body, therefore, you take everything for real and let the problem affect you. Now that you are learning to disidentify from the body, you will not take your issues so seriously. With practice, those problems that come your way will affect you less and less, until they no longer touch you. There is no escape from life's problems, but how you handle them is your call. When you know who you are, you will be able to face any problem head-on, with courage.

Chapter 16.
When the Ego Falls in Love

We buy into love's illusion, hook, line and sinker, even though we know it's not going to last. We hear the same old story replayed time and time again: "He left me... she left me. My life is now over. Look what you've done to me! I'm in pieces, with a glass of shiraz in hand, drowning my sorrows every night. Oh, the pain! I am heartbroken, crying a bucket full of tears".

The despair caused by broken relationships sometimes even leads to suicide. What a complete waste of a life when all this drama is illusory and avoidable! This kind of heart-breaking love springs from body-based attachment. It is not a selfless, free and unconditional love, but rather, a needy and dependent love that comes from seeing oneself as a person! Here, the "I" who has fallen in love is the false ego, which has adopted the body-mind-feelings as its identity. When that ego sees its partner's identity as a body, too, then this love is often unevolved and limited because it is ego-based, with one ego loving another ego. That is duality! Ego-based love is full of wants and needs for itself. Its agenda is one of getting rather than giving.

We are one. There are no "persons" or "personal". There are no separate individuals in Reality. You cannot love anyone else because there is no one else. If there is no other, then consider who is loving whom? If you are not loving your partner, wife or husband, what is going on? You are loving yourself, in your partner. Egoic love is about satisfying one's desires: taking, rather than giving. Personal, self-centred love is not love. However, if the ego is absent, impersonal love is present. This kind of impersonal love is about giving: its nature is expansive and unconditional.

Relationships and family life offer us a great deal of happiness and fulfilment. To avoid falling into their trap and being completely sucked in, we need to be aware of what is going on! We are playing different roles in this dream of life. Establish this fact! Whatever relationship you may be in, whatever role you may be enacting as a lover, wife, husband, mother, father or friend, you are, nonetheless, always role-playing. You are actors, playing different parts in the movie. Don't lose yourself in delusional thinking, believing yourself to be these characters in actuality. Don't be fooled by anything. This life is a dream. Emerge from the dream before it consumes you! Your relationships will not change; they will still be rich and fun-loving. Your perspective will change! And with that shift in perspective, your attachments will loosen naturally and spontaneously.

Chapter 17.
Alienated from Source and Longing to be Whole

You are the Source. When you manifested, you were suddenly separated and disengaged from your Source. And since then, you have been searching for that something that was missing, searching for your absence, searching for a way back Home. You often wanted and needed to engage with something or someone so that you would feel less alienated and more fulfilled. All this time, when you were shopping for lasting happiness and peace and searching for wholeness in the world, you were really longing to rest and abide in your own Source - intrinsic happiness and peace.

Resting in your Source can be compared to the peace and contentment experienced with your true love or soul-partner. You long to be held in your lover's arms and stay there. When you are in the same room with the love of your life, you often don't need to speak because the two, are as if, one, fulfilled and content, just being together in the silence.

Manifesting as the body-form can be compared to the painful wrench caused by an engagement break-up. You were suddenly dumped! Gone was the closeness, that sense of belongingness and security you once experienced. Living the dream suddenly became a living nightmare. You felt alone and broken. All your hopes and wishes of being part of something bigger, and sharing your life with someone, were abruptly and brutally dashed when the rug was cruelly pulled from under your feet. You didn't know if you would ever heal or feel whole again. You wondered if you would ever find that sense of completeness and happiness!

Real, lasting happiness cannot be found in this illusory world. It can only be found in you because you are the Source of happiness and peace. You are the Source of this world. Your nature is peace and bliss. *Sat-chit-ananda* – "Existence-consciousness-bliss", is a classic Sanskrit term that attempts to describe our nature that is beyond words.

Everything is within you. Peace, happiness and love are inbuilt in you as your light-filled, natural state. Your formless nature is perfect love, freedom and bliss. These are not attributes but the very Essence of the Self that you are.

You are Spontaneous Presence

You are that invisible, Spontaneous Presence that has never experienced birth or death. Your existence is eternal. What you are in essence has always existed. It cannot be described for it is no-thing, and yet, it is everything. It is emptiness and it is fullness. Again, the words do not matter, as you are prior to words!

That invisible Reality, that Presence which existed before the body-form will continue its existence after the body-form expires. Let's say there are three movements: No.1. "Omnipresence" is your Stateless State, prior to beingness. No.2. "Spontaneous Presence" emerges from

Omnipresence as your spontaneous manifestation. No.3 Spontaneous Presence merges back into Omnipresence.

The combination of Presence, the elements and consciousness, spontaneously produced the appearance of the body-form. Your Spontaneous Presence emerged without any apparent external cause. Self-generated from the unmanifest to the manifest, from the formless to the form, it came unbidden without any external stimulus, as a natural impulse. Everything unfolded spontaneously: your manifestation, along with the world, which was projected out of your Presence. The nature of our existence is spontaneous and undetermined.

Beyond appearances

The physical world we live in appears to be real, but that is only our perception at work here. Everything is an illusion, emptiness, like atoms. When you stop identifying with the various forms, you will discover that you are the substratum of all shapes and appearances, the very foundation that underlies everything: your appearance and the appearance of the world. The noumenon (the "unseen") is the root of all phenomena (the "seen"). You are that eternal substratum of existence, the invisible Reality and nameless Power or Energy which has been called by many different names: "Ultimate Truth", "Ultimate Reality", "God", etc. That invisible Presence is very subtle, subtler than the sky or space. You are beyond the sky and space because you can see them. You are Reality. Everything is Reality; Reality is everything. You are everything, and everything is in you. Non-duality means that there is only one Reality that is the same in everyone.

The body can function only because of the partnership between Presence and the five-elemental body. Without the power of Presence, it cannot work. It is the combination, spontaneous fusion, that brings about the miracle, fuels the body, and empowers it to operate.

The world which appears to be real is projected from your Presence. Your Spontaneous Presence is the projector. Our mistake was to give importance to the illusory projections instead of the projector. We focussed on the "seen" instead of the "Seer".

Shift your focus

You lived in a state of tension, anxious about something that had happened, or afraid of something that is happening, or something that you think is going to happen. The fact is nothing is going to happen. Nothing has happened and nothing is happening. Because you have taken illusion to be your Reality, you have created a menacing shadow around you, which appears threatening and frightening at times. There will be no need to fear the shadow when you discover that it is yours!

We are all part of one Energy. The world that is projected from this energy is its reflection. It may seem, look, and feel incredibly real, but it is only an appearance! The world is the spontaneous projection of your Spontaneous Presence. All that you see is your reflection. "That" (the unnameable), through which you see is the real deal or bottom line! If life is a movie, you focussed exclusively on the moving images instead of the movie-maker. Or putting it another way, you are not the movie, you are the screen! Shift your focus and stay with the root cause, the Source from which the projection is projected.

Counting the years

Your Presence has always existed. When Presence fused spontaneously with the five elements and you became self-conscious, your problems began. The appearance of the body-form and the world, heralded the beginning of duality. With a click of Presence, the troublesome "I" took birth. You identified with the body-mind complex, measuring your life and counting the years, e.g.: "My age is such and such a number of years. I am a woman who was born in 1981, therefore, my age is forty-one. I am forty-one years of age". There is no woman who is forty-one years old; there is no gender or age. Let go of your identifications with the body-mind, with thought, and all the concepts you have accepted about yourself. You are none of these things. You are part of one Universal Reality.

There are neither women nor men. Prior to beingness, you existed in the Stateless State, as the Stateless State. You were completely unaware – let's say, in holy oblivion - of the complex life in which you now find yourself! During this span of life in the body, you have been under relentless pressures which have caused you anxiety, stress and fear, and sometimes made you feel as if you were living a nightmare. In that nightmare, you sometimes even felt like one of the characters in the movie *Jaws*, running away from gigantic monsters who were intent on catching you, stamping on you and gobbling you up! It is time to get rid of your self-created monsters. Free yourself from all the pressures created by your false identity!

A mirage

The "some-thing" that appeared as a body will disappear one day. It will happen to us all! That some-thing will then merge with no-thing. Put simply, out of nothing, something, (the "body") emerged. Then that something will go back to nothing. Nothing merged with something; something merged with nothing. But there is no something in Reality. That something is an illusion, an appearance, a mirage. Spontaneous Presence is all!

When the Conviction of your Reality arises, you will view everything in a new light and perspective. That Conviction will happen spontaneously. You don't need to use any intellectual effort for that because your

Spontaneous Presence is prior to the intellect! This arising of your Conviction will be spontaneous, in the same way that your Presence arose spontaneously. The nature of Conviction can only be spontaneous because your existence is spontaneous. Your Conviction has nothing to do with reason, logic or cause and effect.

Prior to beingness, your Presence existed. When the body disappears, your Presence will continue to exist. This in-between state where you identified with the body is not your actual state. Now that you know this, you don't need to be so concerned about the illusory body-form and the world, or, with greedy eyes, overfill your pockets on the way! As has been stated many times already, your body will die one day, but you cannot die. Only that which is born can die, and you are unborn! You are, you were, you will always be!

Chapter 18.
No Boundaries

Your Presence, like the sky, is everywhere. If you go to India, Japan, or anywhere else in the world for that matter, your Spontaneous Presence will be right there with you, as you, one with you.

You took yourself to be a human being in charge of your destiny. You are not that! When you take a serious look at yourself, and find out that this world is projected, you will realize your Presence is behind it all, behind everything. You will be given the "Master Key" (a powerful Mantra) to help you turn your attention inwards and unravel the mystery.

We have created the alphabet and language and have assigned meanings to all the different words. Here we are not concerned with words and their definitions, but with Ultimate Reality, the Ultimate Truth that you are, which has nothing to do with words. All this time during your search - whether you knew it or not - you were playing with words, with illusion, with names and forms, trapped in a web of your own making. Reality has nothing to do with words! Wake yourself up! Discriminate! Question everything!

You are the Ultimate Reality. Wherever you go, remember you are Ultimate Reality. When you travel to visit some place or other, it is the body that is transported from A to B; you are not going anywhere. Know that the "Invisible Visitor" in you is the Ultimate Truth. You are always with you. When you know that, really know it deep down, your life will continue to unfold simply, smoothly and stress-free.

Stay with Reality

When your Spirit took form, and you became aware of your existence, the duality began. "Non-duality" means "not two". There is only One Reality. Stay with Reality, and you will find stability and peace. Live as Reality! Be firm, and don't waver! A wavering mind is a dangerous mind that will ruin everything if you give it a chance.

Your Presence is essential, primary. You cannot function without it. There is no power outside of you; there is no additional power besides you! You are everything; you are all! All power is within you. When your body finally disintegrates, who is going to talk about an imaginary, independent power? It's not possible!

These teachings are beyond words, beyond everything. To say that "You are Ultimate Truth" is not just an idea. It is a fact! You are That, without beginning, without end. Who am I? When all the illusory identifications have dissolved, the real "you" will be unveiled. You are formless Reality. What you are hearing is your story. Stay with the Conviction of your Reality, and not just with the words about Reality. The open secret is that you are already "That"! Deepen your

Conviction. You are unborn. Put this knowledge into practice. Absorb it, and enjoy the adventure!

Everything is within You

Now that you know that everything is within you, the focus is shifting from the world to yourself. Look only within; don't look anywhere else. Listen only to yourself; don't listen to anyone else. Read your book! That means you are to go within, look and listen! Your book is the *Book of Answers*. All your questions will be answered from your living fount of knowledge.

You used to think you were in charge, and doing everything. Now you are finding out that everything happens spontaneously, including the appearance of the body-form. A lot of hammering (repetition), is necessary if you are to accept Reality, and begin to alter your entrenched views about yourself, and the world in which you live. You have lived your life with the mistaken notion that you are the body-form, therefore, some resistance is bound to be there. Dropping all your conditioning is not easy, since you have identified with the body-form for so long.

However, as long as your body-based knowledge lingers and the illusory impressions continue to influence you, you will not be able to understand these teachings about your Spontaneous Presence. It is up to you to clear out your old house! In short, the entire world is your spontaneous reflection. There is no "I"; there is no doer. You were never the doer. Without your

Spontaneous Presence, you cannot see, talk or do anything. Begin the rewiring process and change your perspective!

What is the meaning of life?

This life is a long dream! What is the reason for it all? There is no reason. Reason is an intellectual faculty that came along with your bodily existence. Your true nature is spontaneous, prior to reason.

What is the meaning of life? The meaning of life for whom? There is no meaning in life! This is not a nihilistic, pessimistic statement, but the complete opposite which will free you. It will take you out of duality for it takes you beyond the mind, beyond reason and logic. It will lead you to the realization that you are unborn, and the discovery of your true nature, that is Truth, Peace, Bliss and Love. "What is the meaning of life?" is a question, like all your other questions, which arise from a body-based perspective. When you no longer perceive yourself from that perspective, you will no longer have any questions.

What was your identity prior to the body-form, and what will it be when you leave the body? Contemplate on that, instead of trying to find meaning in your dream life. Ignore the words such as "meaning", "life", "death", "aims", "goals", "language", etc. They have nothing to do with your real identity. You have a golden opportunity to awaken from the dream! That is all there is to say about your dream life.

Your Presence existed prior to beingness, prior to the mind, the ego, and the intellect. Why this life? Don't look for a "Why?" Don't look for a reason why Presence took form. Call it a mystery! There is no reason at all. The body is not your identity and it will not remain your identity because it is only a brief, spontaneous appearance. Reality is beyond the grasp and capabilities of the intellect and imagination. You can only experience it. That is "your" proof. You are the Final Truth. The entire world is projected out of your Spontaneous Presence, and the same thing will happen in reverse when the projected world withdraws. Let Reality find you!

We all have deeply ingrained tendencies to apply reason and logic to our lives because we identified with the body-form. Work on shovelling out these tendencies, little by little. Reality has nothing to do with reason and logic.

Chapter 19.
"I Don't Know"

We do not know why we manifested, or the way we were prior to manifestation. It is humbling to realize that we don't have all the answers. (It seems that scientists have also hit a wall in their research into "Consciousness". They have not been able to locate or explain the nature of consciousness!)

As much as we would like to find out what it was like prior to beingness, we will not be able to know. How can we expect to know the infinite, the eternal, using finite tools, such as the mind, the intellect, logic and imagination? How can our limited minds possibly know the unlimited? How can the mind know that which is prior to it? It's an impossibility!

If one were to try to describe the Stateless State prior to beingness, the only words one can use, the only appropriate words are: "I don't know". "I don't know" is the only response, the perfect answer. All you can know about your formless Selfless Self is "I don't know".

That "I don't know" appears to be a "negative" answer, but it's not. It comes from a "positive". "I don't know" means, "I know!" I know I did not exist in any kind of form because I did not know myself prior to beingness! The knowing is the Presence, the "I am". You know, that you don't know. All you can say about "prior to beingness", therefore, is "I don't know". After leaving behind the body, what will you be like? Again, all you can say is, "I don't know". Be as you are prior to beingness! Dwell in "I don't know".

Temporary blindness

When the body-form covered over your Spirit-Presence, your original nature was temporarily hidden from view. However, now that you are waking up, the Light is beginning to peek through.

Ignore what is to be ignored and keep your attention focussed on the Source. Remould yourself! Look after your sensitive, impressionable Spirit. If you give your attention to everything that is happening in this imaginary world, you will end up seriously depressed, or even a little crazy. Be Self-attentive! Be a Master of this world; you are not its slave.

Keep deflating the ego. Forget about everything you once thought you were and let Spirit shine through, clear and bright. When your Inner Listener is reminded of its own story, it is warmed, as if hugged and kissed from the inside.

You are no longer blind! Reality has refreshed the memory of your identity, prompting you to "see" again.

Return journey home

To truly know who we are, we need to return Home. How do we get back Home? By returning to that "I don't know", Stateless State. That will happen when all the information we have accepted throughout our lives dissolves. The Knowledge and the simple Practices presented here are both practical and efficient. Their power will decimate the attachments we have accumulated throughout our lives, along with the rest of our baggage.

Your intellect alone will not assist you in your quest to know yourself directly. Neither will the majority of books, or the finest literature, as they originated in the manifest world. They will not give you direct knowledge. Reading this Knowledge is the first step of the great undoing, the dynamite, that will blow up your illusory knowledge. Using the Practice Tools is the second step, to help you absorb the Knowledge.

If a gardener intends to grow flowers, he will do four things: Clear the ground, plant the seeds, water them and let them grow. Here the process from illusion to Reality requires a similar progression: Clear out the illusory concepts, accept the knowledge of Reality, reflect and absorb Reality, and don't interfere. Let Reality unfold spontaneously! Be patient like the gardener. Watch and wait!

You searched for Truth because you had forgotten your true identity. When you have removed all the false knowledge, Eureka! Your identity will be revealed! That is a big moment. There you are, unveiled! There you are, as you have always been, and as you will always be - Formless Reality! You are that silent, Supreme Being, the Absolute, Presence, Energy, Power, Divinity, God, or any other name you wish to use. You are not separate or different from what we call "God". That Godly Essence is one and the same within us all.

You are a Power House

Your Presence, that Divine, Godly Essence, has never experienced individuality. The body is not ultimate; Presence is ultimate. When that spark of Presence leaves the body and again merges with Omnipresence, the body dies. You may not have the "X-Factor", but you have the "God-Factor"! Now that you know the true value of this passing body, use it to "know thyself".

You are omnipresent God that is everywhere like the sky or space. To know this directly, first-hand, you need to carry on sweeping away all the traces of falsehood. Don't be impatient! It has taken you years to construct your house. Persevere! Keep chipping away at King Ego, removing his pride, jealousy, praises, bruises, likes, dislikes, etc. Identify who, or what, is still in your head that should not be there!

After a thorough "spring clean", your environment will be less cluttered. Little by little, your Reality will reveal itself in this fresh expanse of space, allowing you to look, see and discover your immensity and power. Spend time with yourself! It is only when you are Self-attentive and Self-involved that you can tap into the Source that you are.

Chapter 20:
No Religion Except Self-Realization

Before beingness there was no such thing as religion, spirituality or God-talk. What is the purpose of belonging to a particular religion? What use does this kind of knowledge have? Religions offer manmade, artificial knowledge, meanings and interpretations. In other words, further, false layers of identity. The concept of religion did not exist before beingness.

Sadly, the principle of religion, namely, transcendence and feelings of unity, was submerged a long time ago. It is not surprising that religion has gone out of fashion. High-standing priests and ministers of various religions, institutions and organizations, have been abusing their powers. These representatives (of God) have not been acting as mediators but have, instead, been standing in our way, keeping us ignorant, dependent and powerless. They have been blocking us from the direct knowledge of our Truth and Reality!

Some of you may have visited churches or temples in the past, to petition God and ask for blessings. When you come to know that you are not separate from God, that you are that Godly Essence, you will realize that no one can bless you except yourself! That is not an arrogant statement of the ego talking. When you know you are All, both immanent and transcendent, when your true nature finally dawns on you, you will feel the urge to bow to that Presence within you and bless yourself. There is no religion except Self-Realization! We have only one duty in this life: to investigate and find out who we are. Be passionate. Enjoy this magnificent opportunity!

Throw out the concepts

Rid yourself of those deeply ingrained notions that some of you may have been carrying around for a while. It is said that God made us in his image. This is another fairy story. We have made God in our image! There is no "Creator God"; God is not separate from you.

Some people revere the holy books, bow to the bishops, and pray to a mythical God in the sky as they were taught to do. Who created this version of "God"? We did! We know that there was no knowledge prior to beingness, therefore, there was no knowledge of "God" either.

There is no God, except "Formless You". There is no God that is separate from you. God is the name we give to the Divine Energy which powers everything. But what you maybe missed or didn't realize, is that this Power or Divine Energy is yours. That Power is your Power!

Where is God?

Some of us may have been searching for God out there, hoping and searching for a celestial God who was running the show, ruling the entire world, punishing some and blessing others on the way. No one has ever seen God because that Godly Essence is within the "Seer", within you! You cannot see "God" because you are "God", the ineffable.

Our need for God only arose alongside our many other requirements when we took form. The word G.O.D is no different from the rest of the vocabulary we conjured up. Hard as you may try, you will not be able to find a God with a separate existence from you, anywhere. Everything is within you. Nothing exists that is separate from you. You are the All!

Your origin

Shift your perspective to "prior to beingness" and meditate! You will "get it" through meditation. Drop the concepts! Contemplate! Take up your position on higher ground and abide there, free of all concepts, ideas, images - of woman, man, human being, mind, ego, self, no self, God, etc. Drop all the misunderstandings surrounding "God". The concepts of pain and a Creator God who allows pain are untrue and unnecessarily harmful. There is no God except your formless, Selfless Self. Identify God within you! Everything is to be found in you. You are Almighty God! You are Ultimate Truth! Stand in your Power!

Knowledge has a place only because of the body-form's needs. In Reality, where nothing and nobody exists, there are neither needs, nor any place for a fairy tale God! The concept of God is just that, a concept, an illusion. Spirituality, too, is an illusion, a thorn, whose sole function it is to remove the primary, illusory thorn of "I am the body". Once this has been accomplished, you can also dispense with the thorn of spirituality.

Reality, not spirituality

I hear some of you baulking at the mention of the word "God". *What's God gotta do with it?* You may say: "I am not a spiritual person! I don't believe in that kind of thing. I don't have any faith". I'm not religious, etc., etc.". That's absolutely fine, even better! This knowledge is universal knowledge that has nothing to do with spirituality, faith, religion, or belief systems whatsoever. What is presented here are the facts of your existence: Your Reality, One Reality. What is shared here is the true story of our Universal Reality. We are One! We are one Essence.

Forget about the concept of spirituality! We live in an age of science and rationality. We remain uninterested unless something can be explained logically. Let's take another quick look at your identity! Step back and distance yourself for a moment. Seriously consider the following: at the beginning of your bodily life, you were a baby, a young child. Then you started to grow up, moving through the different stages of adolescence, teenage years, adulthood and, for some readers, old age. Can you honestly say, or think, that this body-form which is constantly changing, is your actual identity?

Can you take on board and accept that you are a temporary, impermanent body-form? How can impermanence be your Reality?

Fact – you are immortal

It is a fact that you are immortal. Your Presence has always been in existence and it will always continue its existence! It was there prior to the body-form, and it will be there after the body-form expires. It is here now as the "holder", the "sustainer" of your body. The visible is false; the invisible is true. Or, putting it another way, the visible is secondary (relative reality) because it is a reflection of the Source, that is primary, (Absolute Reality) – all One and the same Reality! Whatever experiences you may have had throughout life, know that you remain eternally untouched. The permanent does not change; it will always just be as it is. Discriminate, and love the permanent!

You are prior to beingness; you are after beingness. Whatever we see in-between, during our material existence, is the projection, the reflection of your Spontaneous Presence. Whatever is experienced by you is spontaneously created. It is your projection because as you know, you cannot experience anything without your Presence. These Teachings, (along with the recommended Practices), will lead to spontaneous Self-realization, which is not an intellectual realization, but experiential. It occurs once the knowledge has been fully absorbed.

Now you are laughing!

At some point, you will come to realize that the heavy baggage of dread and trepidation surrounding your mortality, which you may have carried around for decades, was utterly unnecessary. When you know that you expended so much energy trying to keep at bay a gigantic monster, that never existed in the first place, you will burst into paroxysms of laughter. Some people even opt for cryogenics in their desperation to conquer death! This beast, or demon of death, never existed in the first place. Oh well! You can now let go of the big "D" as well!

Self-enquiry leads to Self-knowledge. Self-knowledge leads to Self-realization. Genuine Self-knowledge is essential, for without it, the end of the bodily life will most likely be distressing and painful. If you have any lingering fears around death, keep at it! Continue Self-enquiring. Unearth everything, e.g., conditioning around the subject of death, trauma, grief, etc. Expose your weak spots. Unless you have examined yourself thoroughly, your fears will continue to hover around you. All thoughts and concepts are untrue. Fear is untrue! Fear is nothing but a scary bluff that comes from the ego.

Find out who you are! Die to the ego before the body dies! This fundamental and pragmatic knowledge is like an insurance policy that will guarantee you a fearless state when the body dies. Prepare yourself for a smooth transition at the end of your bodily life. If you awaken to your Reality now, that moment of separation from the body will not only be smooth but an incredibly beautiful, peaceful and blissful one.

Settling your affairs does not only mean drawing up a Will and dividing your Estate. More importantly, it is about realizing that you never owned anything in the first place, and letting go of everything.

When you know what you are, the questions you had about death will never arise again. And when your time comes, you will be armed with a fear-proof vest of courage. When you are fearless at the end, completely fearless, that is absolute Conviction, the ultimate sign of established knowledge!

Energy cannot be lost

In this dream world, you celebrate your family members' birthdays and mourn their deaths. Whose birthday party are you attending? There is no birth. Whose funeral are you attending? There is no death. Energy cannot be lost; it can only be transmuted! The cemeteries are full of monuments erected to loved ones. But they were never born, and they never died. Whose wedding are you attending? Who is marrying whom? This world is an illusion, a dream. Think about it! It is a dream for the "unborn child". You are celebrating and mourning the unborn child. Knowing this, however, is never to be used as an excuse for insensitive behaviour. Always be compassionate towards the bereaved!

Keep absorbing this knowledge! The world and everyone you know and everything in it, is just a dream. Its brief appearance was always destined to disappear. Not you, however. You are permanent. You are unborn!

Chapter 21.
Knowledge for the Unborn Child

You are unborn. You are that child who was never born. What is there to say about an unborn child except that nothing happened, nothing is happening, and nothing is ever going to happen? When you begin to see through the mirage, and swap your rose-tinted spectacles for divinely designed ones, you will no longer see duality. You will see only Oneness. Then you will be able to navigate your way through life quickly, easily and spontaneously, seeing with the eye of knowledge. This knowledge is for the unborn child who imagined she was born.

Living as disconnected-from-Source, separate individuals is tough and challenging. No wonder we needed all sorts of knowledge and philosophies to give us a little peace and happiness. We may have encountered many methods and paths: intellectual, metaphysical, scientific, humanistic, philosophy, spirituality and religion. There is Buddhism, Zen, Sufism and all sorts of systems. However, now that you know yourself better, you will not have the same inclination to go after knowledge from philosophy, psychology, theology, or continue to search for other methods, paths or ways. Your identity is beyond human-made dogmas, "isms", or "ologies". Your identity does not lie within any of these. You are always identity-less!

Be mindful without the mind

An overdose of worldly knowledge has served only to reinforce duality, tribalism and separation. There is only one Source, one Reality, Universal Reality. You are That!

Some books address the tremendous fear around the concepts of death, guilt, good/bad, sin/merit, heaven/hell etc. These ingrained concepts have caused intense grief to many, and yet, we did not know anything about them in our Stateless State, prior to beingness. Our illusory body-forms acquired all this illusory knowledge because we were lost in the world and alienated from our Source.

Your Presence is effortless, without any adjuncts, concepts, imagination, guesswork or any intellectual activity at all. After Self-Realization, there won't be any stress, dis-ease, unhappiness or fear at all because you will have realized, "I am unborn". (No one realizes. Self-Realization happens when "you", the ego-mind, is extinguished.) Wherever you are, you will know who, or what, you are - Ultimate Truth. You will be mindful without the mind!

Taste the nectar of Beloved-Presence

If lasting happiness can only be found in you, get used to spending quality time with yourself. First, be still for five minutes, then, ten, fifteen, twenty, gently increasing the duration every few days. Fix your attention on Selfless Self. As you go deeper, you will forget about time because you are Self-absorbed, enjoying timeless peace and stillness.

If you achieve some kind of success in life or go through a rite of passage, you will experience transient pleasure. But when you taste the indescribable nectar of Presence, you will be filled with lasting, profound contentment and substantial joy.

When you arrive at the Truth of "Who am I?", you will have fewer desires. By that time, you will know that everything can be found in you because you alone are the real deal! You will not be hungry for more money, or obsessed with moving into a bigger house. You will not be so interested in the world, or in seeking happiness from material things, because you will know better! Some of you will even be able to avoid the concept of a "mid-life crisis" - if that is still on the cards - now that you know you are the Source of happiness. Happiness is your nature - permanent, causeless happiness, that just is.

On your way Home

Stick with Reality instead of fleeting materiality. You are in the process of finding out who you are. The discomfort, unease and pain you may have been carrying are dissolving. You are on your way back Home to the Source.

Be devoted to uncovering your Source, Essence, light, peace, happiness, love. Devotion is not something holy or the worship of something other. It is not observance or sanctity, but a practice that is dedicated and committed to finding your Truth. Self-devotion is the ultimate love affair: the union of the "Lover and the Beloved", Oneness.

As the seeker tracks down the sought-after, she can sometimes experience a sort of impassioned madness. The seeker may have intense experiences of heightened warmth, burning Truth and profound intimacy, like "lying on a bed of bliss, 24/7". Knowing and being will draw closer and closer to one another, until eventually, they merge as one, beyond knowingness, beyond beingness. You will know what you are, and you will be what you know! It happens!

Absorption

You may have some doubts. You may feel unsure, even a little scared-off which make it difficult for you to accept these teachings. But you already take so much on trust, so why not take this on trust, too? What do you have to lose? Even if you feel unable to accept what you have read just now, the Truth of your existence is still working its magic, and continuing to drill through the walls of your resistance. The spontaneous process of Self-Realization has begun. It cannot be reversed. When the Conviction arises spontaneously, you will realize that you were never in bondage. You have always been free and infinite.

Reading these Teachings is not enough in itself. Practice is essential to purify, disempower the mind and hammer the ego. Without that, these Teachings will not be pragmatic. You can listen to different teachers, podcasts or seminars, "till the cows come home", but without meditation, you will not be able to know yourself directly. You will only be able to know yourself through words that keep feeding the ego.

The Knowledge and the Practice together – both are essential to take you out of the "Dark Night of the Ego" and lead you to the "Living Light of Love".

Absorb this Knowledge completely with every fibre of your being! It needs to be absorbed completely. How? By attending Bootcamp, where you will learn the essential "Tools" of "Self-Enquiry", "Mantra", "Meditation", and "Kirtan".

Part Four: Bootcamp

"Let silence be the art you practice." Rumi

Chapter 22.
The Practice – Your Toolkit

At Bootcamp, you will receive your very own "Bespoke Toolkit", which will equip you with the essential resources needed for Self-Realization. Here, you will receive tough, practical training. As you undergo the process, you will undo and remove all the illusory layers and add-ons that have attached themselves to your Presence. First of all, you need to clear the cluttered, overgrown path, strewn with the weeds of socialization. Remove the thoughts, ideas, points of view, stances, impressions – all of them were acquired by society. It is essential that the ground is completely cleared and cleaned before planting any seeds. Nothing will grow in the soil, unless you root out all the weeds produced from ignorance that were taking up your precious space. Sweep away all these fake seeds because they are not part of your essential nature. They are not part of who you are, and are preventing the flower of Truth from blossoming.

This knowledge of your Reality is straightforward, but absorbing and living as that Reality is a little more challenging. We know that nothing worth doing is ever easy! How can we embed this knowledge so that it can be of practical use in our daily lives? We can do this by enrolling at Bootcamp and learning the trade!

Embedding the Knowledge

Every trade has its tools. In order to know who or what you are, to truly understand and know our real nature, we also need to use some tools such as "Self-enquiry", "Reciting a Mantra", "Meditating", and "Singing/Chanting or listening to Kirtans". This practice, like everything else, is an illusion. However, it is vital in the beginning - like serving an apprenticeship where you undergo proper training to learn the relevant skills that will make you proficient. Here you will immerse yourself in the Practices till you are match-fit, until the techniques become so automatic, that they eventually continue by themselves. Bootcamp works!

The practice of Self-enquiry is essential for you to find out first-hand, what you are not. Then you can remove everything about yourself that is not true.

The Mantra's job is one of hammering the ego. A mantra is a concentration tool that weakens the resistant mind. Reciting a mantra lets the mind know who is in charge and running the whole show, i.e., the authentic ruler!

Meditation is necessary to establish your Reality. Here, basic meditation involves churning the knowledge of your Reality – that you are unborn, limitless, the Source, prior to beingness, etc. - and not letting your concentration stray. It means keeping your attention fixed on your Reality, until that Ultimate Reality that you are is permanently established. When this happens, you will no longer need to put in any effort.

Song and chant and/or listening to kirtans will also help you to absorb the knowledge. It is another effective medium to keep the thoughts at bay, while at the same time creating and maintaining, a happy and uplifting atmosphere.

Together, these tools work to remove all the illusory layers, similar to the way a potent cocktail removes our inhibitions! The overall aim is to supplant the idea, the false notion of "I am the body", with the Truth of "I am Ultimate Reality". If this Truth just remains an idea or theoretical, it will not work. There has to be a deep and direct Conviction leading to the direct experience of your Truth. In other words, there must be total acceptance. All these aids are necessary to kick the old tenants out of your house, bring about a successful shift in perspective, and eventually, take you out of duality.

Beingness is unbearable

When the Spirit-Presence touched with the body, you appeared as a "human being". It was a traumatic event. The child cries because she cannot explain or make sense of what is going on. Confused and fearful, she does not understand why she has so many needs!

At some stage in your life, you may have felt a little lost. Not knowing who you were, where you had come from or where you were going, you found yourself drowning in a deep sea of intense feelings of lostness and aloneness. In time, this led to the following dilemma: "Who am I? I am in a body, but if the body is not my identity, then who am I?" This is the root of Self-Enquiry. You are trying to find the answer to the big question, "Who/what am I?"

When you were trapped in the imaginary world, you identified with people, places and things which kept you in a constant state of flux. You became slaves of the mind, the ego, and the intellect. These tenants took over your house, living there like squatters and draining you of all your energy and power. It is time to evict them! It is time to stop listening to these old records, and go against the flow. You don't have to let the winds of change pull you here and there. You don't have to follow the mind. Turn it around and develop the habit of letting the mind follow you! Bootcamp's primary aim is to disempower the mind and reveal your Original, Stateless State: You are unborn. You are before beingness!

Recovery

When you eventually wake up and realize that everything is an illusion, all your suffering will come to an end. Be patient and strong! The rigours at Bootcamp are challenging. It takes time to overcome the early trauma of separation from the Source, of disconnectedness, alienation, the sense of something missing, of unbelonging. Its long-term effects are like PTSD (post-traumatic stress disorder). Not to worry though! These symptoms will gradually lessen and they will vanish eventually.

Attending Bootcamp can be compared to an admission to a rehab clinic, to detox and address an addiction. If one is an alcoholic, the toxins first need to be removed from the body. Then one needs to understand the issues that led to the addiction and learn new ways of living healthily - i.e., free from that addiction. In the context of Self-Realization, identification with the body-mind complex led to an addiction, the craving for sensual pleasures and taking the world for real. Understanding the issues around this addiction means looking at one's ignorance and gaining Self-knowledge. Learning new ways of living means carrying out the practice, which will eventually lead you back to your original, unborn Selfless Self.

Chapter 23.
Self-Enquiry – Examine yourself

What is Self-enquiry? How do you practice it? Ask yourself the question, "Who am I?" "Who am I?" is really "What am I?" as there is no "Who?" that is an individual entity or personal self. But then again, there is no "What?" either, as there is "no-thing" to find! The purpose of Self-enquiry is to examine yourself and find out what you are not, by undergoing a process of negation. So, how do we practise Self-enquiry? We do it by using discrimination and deconstructing all that we think we are! Look for the constant! Look for the permanent!

Begin by asking yourself, "Am I the body?" You cannot be the body because you have observed it and can quickly see how your body has changed consistently, from the time you were a little child, until the way it is now, as a fully-grown adult! You cannot be the body.

Are you the mind? As we have seen, the mind is simply the flow of thoughts. "Am I my thoughts?" With a little reflection, you will know that you cannot be your thoughts because you can observe and see that they are always in flux, coming and going, rising and falling - whereas you do not come and go!

Repeat the exercise once more, this time regarding your feelings and emotions. Again, you will know that your feelings do not define what you are, for they, too, appear and disappear. You can observe and see them constantly changing. You know this from your own experiences, when you feel happy one moment, and then sad or angry, the next. Our moods change all the time, from elation to depression, excitement to boredom, etc. Everything that changes is not you. You are not the changing waves of emotion. The real you does not change!

You are not your experiences

Are you your experiences? What if you are a combination, the totality of all your life's experiences? Is it possible that everything that has happened to you, your whole life story, including all the thoughts, feelings, wants and needs, memories, etc., might be who you are? Could that be it? No! Because there is something that is always observing, that sees everything. There is something that witnesses all your experiences that make up the movie of your life! So, you cannot be your experiences either. You are beyond your experiences because you can witness them all the time! Keep going! The next step is to find out if you are the "witness". Track down the witness!

Where can you find this witness? You investigate a little more deeply, but you cannot find it. "Who is this witness? What is this witness?" You examine yourself, pondering, wondering if this might be what you have been looking for all this time. But hard as you try, you realize that you cannot identify the witness. You still don't know. It is a big mystery! You cannot find yourself! It feels like you have reached a dead end. You have not! You cannot identify yourself because anything you can locate must be an object, and you are not an object! Your identity is an invisible, anonymous identity.

Beyond identification

The practice of Self-enquiry will not give you a pat answer, such as, "Eureka! I am Joe Bloggs!" You won't find a solution to "Who am I?" because you are the subject of the investigation. If you still feel that you need an answer, all that can be said in response to "Who am I?" is, the "Invisible Questioner is the answer". What does that mean? It means that when you pose this question, you, or your invisible identity, are That which you are seeking, without words. The Investigator is the subject of enquiry which is looking for Itself. What you are cannot be an object.

Who am I? Who is living and who is dying? No one! You are not a person. You are participating in a long dream in which you are playing various roles at different times. So, who am I? You are beyond labels!

You may feel frustrated now and conclude that Self-enquiry is a pointless exercise. You hoped for, wanted, and even expected to find some concrete answers. On the contrary, it is not pointless as the practice teaches you how to stop playing that particular mind-game. It is not futile because it teaches you how to bring all of your false identifications to an end. When you can be the watcher of your dream movie, merely looking at what appears to be happening, then you will be liberated from the confines of being an individual, who is always entangled in an illusory something or someone!

Stand guard!

Asking the question, "Who am I?" is the most critical question you can ask because it opens the door to the Infinite. When you sift through all of your concepts, shake them up and loosen your attachments to the false and the transient, then your natural, endless Source will open up and reveal itself. Self-enquiry helps to shift your attention from the imaginary world of the seen, to the Seer. It removes the obstacles that are taking up space and cluttering up your vastness: the incessant noise of the mind that prevents you from hearing the silence. When that disturbing hum stops and the thoughts lessen, a pure and beautiful silent space will emerge.

Self-enquiry is particularly useful at the beginning of the process of dismantling all the ideas and notions you have about yourself. Get into the habit of standing guard and intercepting the thoughts as they arise. While we cannot stop the thoughts from flowing, as that is the nature of the mind, nevertheless, we can stop them in their tracks before they have had a chance to leave their impressions, or begin to multiply.

It is a matter of being aware and keeping watch, so that when you see your attention going outwards, you can rein it back in. When you don't entertain the thoughts by not letting them in, they will just dissolve. Don't take delivery! How do you intercept your thoughts? You can do it by asking the question, "To whom does this thought arise?" followed by "To me". This simple and effective exercise reminds you that you are not the arising thought. It breaks up the flow, and quickly disempowers it, stopping you from being swept along by it. When thoughts are arrested in this way, they will simply fall away. Be vigilant, and in particular, be on the lookout for apparently new and exciting thoughts, or ideas that attempt to snare you, and pull you back into the world of illusion!

Catch them before they catch you

Catch the thoughts before they catch you! Make Self-enquiry a habit. It will soon get easier with practice. You can also intercept those irritating or troublesome thoughts that remind you of your worldly problems, such as work, relationship issues and/or money worries. You can prevent these from developing further, by posing the simple question: "Was this problem there prior to beingness?" Or, "Where was this problem, prior to beingness?" Asking these questions will dissolve the thoughts and disarm them of power.

Each and every one of our thoughts, ideas, concepts and problems are imaginary. They were not there prior to beingness, prior to the body-mind appearance. Therefore, posing the question: "Was this problem there prior to beingness?" is a useful and constant reminder of your true nature. Use it as a barometer for those times when you "forget", let down your guard, and find yourself caught up in problems again! Remember that peace is always there, unless you disturb it! Stay with that peace. Stay as that peace!

Starve the ego

What are the aims of the Self-Enquiry process? Self-Enquiry frees us from our illusory, mental prisons, disempowers and reduces our thoughts and brings about the disappearance of the illusory thinker. That primary "I-thought" (mind/ego) is the culprit responsible for identifying with all the thoughts and concepts. It is the hook on which all the other thoughts and ideas hang. That pseudo-ego has only managed to survive because we have been giving all our attention and interest to the thoughts, without any discrimination. All thought is unreal, and all thought is fleeting. You are prior to thought, prior to words.

How will you know when you have made progress? The answer is: when the thoughts drop off, and the thinker dissolves. When you expose the pseudo "I", your identification with the body-form will cease. When it is finally rooted out, there will no longer be a hook on which to hang any thoughts. When the illusion dissolves, there will no longer be a phantom ego that has been posing as a Master, for you, its slave, to serve. When witnessing is all that remains, and you no longer identify with anything, that is progress! Don't try to grasp what is happening. Don't get carried away or adopt a new identity, such as "I am enlightened" or "I am Self-Realized!" Remember that you are, before and beyond words!

Hitting a wall

You are beyond understanding, therefore, don't look for an answer that can be put into words, or a solution you can understand, because anything you can understand is not who you are! You are unfathomable! How can our conditioned, limited minds understand the Absolute! Self-enquiry will inevitably lead you to a wall, to the answer, "I don't know!"

When you accept this answer, you have reached a significant landmark. Then you will be able to focus your attention on the pure Self that is Selfless Self, without any add-ons! You are a mystery, a wonder, beyond both reason and imagination. To know that the mind is incapable of giving you the answers you have been looking for is both liberating and humbling! When you hit this wall, you are acknowledging, not even acknowledging, but you know, that you are beyond all that you can conceive of, or perceive. And, more than that, there is the recognition of something greater than your limited body-mind, a recognition of your transcendent nature, that impersonal, Universal Self, Oneness.

You cannot use a method to find out what you are, however, Self-enquiry removes the obstacles on the path - i.e., eliminating, one by one, what you are not. After all the layers have been removed, what is left is what you are: the unknowable, the unnameable. When you understand that you are beyond understanding, you can surrender to the unknown! And when that vastness opens up, peace, happiness and bliss will start flowing.

We are always looking elsewhere for knowledge and information from books, others, and various websites. When you read books, you are adding further layers of material knowledge, second-hand knowledge. True knowledge is Self-Knowledge. Go within, and read your own book, *Who am I?* See what is inside, and there you will find what you are looking for: stillness, peace, happiness and love. With intensive re-training, you will learn to stand on your own two feet and rely on others less and less. You will start surfing the web, your very own website of Selfless Self, and get to know who you are directly and inside out, without words!

Chapter 24.
Mantra – The Master Key

The word "Mantra" has been adopted by contemporary culture as a sort of motivating chant or self-affirming statement, such as, for example, "I can and I will. I can and I will". Or "I am not afraid to be wrong. I am not afraid to be wrong". There are happiness mantras, based on the idea that we can choose to attract happiness, like the mantra: "I create my path and walk it with joy", or, "I change my thoughts, I change my world". These mantras are no different to those popular mottos which are repeated over and over again, until whoever is saying them, really believes in them. For example, the late Steve Jobs used the mantra, "Better never than late", which emphasized quality over quantity. Oprah Winfrey's mantra of choice is: "Everything is always working out for me!" However, these modern-day aphorisms are not proper mantras, in the same way that "fashion gurus" are not real gurus!

Mantras can be found in every tradition, from the ancient *"Om/Aum"* mantra to Transcendental Meditation (TM) mantras, from the "Jesus Prayer" in Christianity to Hebrew mantra/prayers. Many celebrity converts to traditions such as Hinduism or Buddhism have been instrumental in raising the profile of mantra meditation. E.g., Richard Gere is a long-standing Buddhist practitioner. In contrast, Tina Turner is affiliated with Japanese Nichiren Buddhism. Singer-songwriter Miley Cyrus and actress Julia Roberts both turned to Hinduism for their practice, to mention but a few of them!

TM is practised by many throughout the world, including the actor Jim Carrey, record producer Rick Rubin, filmmaker David Lynch, singer/songwriter Donovan, TV host, actress Ellen DeGeneres, etc.

Many of us are already familiar with the mantra "*Om*" and its symbol, which is frequently used commercially in art, jewellery, T-shirts, etc. This esoteric syllable is considered to be the most sacred mantra in Hinduism and Tibetan Buddhism. "*Om*", which symbolically embodies the divine energy, is described as the "unstruck sound", the primordial sound, from which the whole universe was created. You may have chanted it at the beginning and end of a yoga class. Some of the most well-known mantras are Tibetan Buddhism's "*Om Mani Padme Hum.* Japanese Buddhism's "*Namu Myoho Renge Kyo*", and the Hindu/Sanskrit "*Soham*", *Tat Tvam Asi*, "*Aham Brahmasmi*".

So, what is the purpose of the mantra? The mantra is a vehicle or instrument that transports us beyond thought. At a basic, health-giving level, mantra practices promote calm and reduce stress. However, our aim here is to use an effective mantra primarily as a concentration tool that will reduce much more than stress! Alongside our other practices, we will use a mantra to disempower the mind, eliminate illusion, and establish ourselves in our true nature.

Mantra - bring in the pest control!

The old tenants, namely, the mind, ego and the intellect, are unruly. We need some assistance to blast them out of their comfortable dwelling place. We need to bring in the pest control to make the environment unbearable for them. Here, the pest control takes the form of Mantra Meditation/Recitation. This practice will enable a thorough cleaning process to take place.

The simple reciting of a mantra will be used for as long as it takes to decondition and wash the brain from a lifetime's brainwashing. We will use the mantra, *"Aham Brahmasmi"*.

Two thorns

You can view a mantra as the thorn that will remove the existing, unwanted thorn. The current thorn is "I am the body" (and its replacement is "I am Ultimate Reality"). The continuous reciting of a mantra hammers the ego and effectively dissolves body-based knowledge, eventually establishing you as Ultimate Reality.

Start using the mantra now, mentally reciting, *"Aham Brahmasmi"*. *Aham* means "I am"; *Brahmasmi* refers to pure existence. This mantra means, "the core of my Being is the Ultimate Reality, the root and ground of the universe, the source of all that exists. I am infinite Reality". When you recite this mantra, you are invoking the Presence, the Reality. If you prefer to say it in

English, use "I am *Brahman. Brahman* I am" (again, mentally), to hammer the ego. Put simply, the meaning of the mantra is "I am Ultimate Reality. Ultimate Reality I am". The little, illusory "i" and the big "I" of Truth cannot coexist! You could say that the mantra's power quashes the small "i", along with all its mistaken notions, so that the big "I" can be re-established.

Reciting this mantra is a simple technique that reminds you of your forgotten identity. It dislodges the mistaken concepts such as woman, man, non-binary, etc, and replaces these with your real identity.

This kind of hammering or repetition of your Reality establishes you in your Truth. You are at the destination. Truth is within you. You are the destination! Your involvement and commitment to this training are essential to enable you to discriminate between the false and the real. Eventually, you will realize that nothing exists except Selfless Self. There is nothing apart from Selfless Self. There is only one Principle. You are That!

Master Key

The mantra *Aham Brahmasmi* is a sacred utterance, a numinous sound, where the vibration and the meaning are the same. Using this practice, will help take you out of illusion and eventually pave your way back Home. This corrective process acts as a constant reminder of who/what you are. Reciting this mantra will dissolve your strong thoughts and concepts, melting the remnants of the illusory you, who still thinks yourself to be somebody! Let the anti-virus do its thing and uproot all your buried hurts and memories of, e.g., anger, violation, betrayal, injustice etc. Put an end to your suffering by disidentifying with the body-form, and going beyond your illusory wounds and scars.

Say, for example, that in the past, you were diagnosed with cancer or had been involved in a serious accident. Even long after your healing, the events left you with lasting impressions. However, when you no longer identify with the body-form, you will see that cancer or an accident affects only the body – it does not affect "you"!

Reciting a mantra is a simple antidote to illusion. How does the mantra *Aham Brahmasmi* work? It engages the mind and stops the activity. Intellectual and egoistic activity stop spontaneously with the reciting of the mantra. At the same time, Spirit-Presence begins to flow outwards, as it is reminded of its identity, its Reality. When you adopt this practice, the mind quietens down, and a peaceful space comes to the fore. Don't strain your brain trying to understand how it works, or if it is working at all, just continue to recite the mantra, with total commitment and concentration.

Establishing a routine

You will need to put in some effort and discipline in the beginning. Recite the mantra, (mentally at all times), for two hours per day, divided into two one-hour sessions, or four, at half an hour! When you give the practice your full attention, this is known as concentrated recitation.

Sit comfortably! There is no need for you to try and sit crossed-legged like a *yogi*, especially if it will cause you pain that will inevitably distract you from the practice. You can either close your eyes, or, if you find concentration difficult, half-close your eyes and focus on the tip of your nose. Inhale as you recite the first part of the mantra, "*Aham*", and exhale with the second part, "*Brahmasmi*".

In addition to this practice, mentally recite the mantra, (without the inhale/exhale), while you are attending to various chores and activities, such as walking, cooking, cleaning, showering, etc. This kind of approach will ensure that the mantra steadily becomes part of your daily routine. And as a result, it will embed your Reality within you quickly. After some time, you may begin to notice the mantra continuing on its own, spontaneously reciting, by itself in the background.

Commit to the practice and give it your undivided attention. Concentration with total involvement, deep involvement, is essential. Use the mantra forcefully like a battering ram to crush King Ego, and open the door to your Source, Queen Bliss. Mantras are Master Keys, entry passes to your House of Self-knowledge. Your resolve and determination to find out "Who am I?" is what matters here. Throw yourself into the practice unreservedly!

Chapter 25.
No Gain Without Pain!

At first, the mind, ego and intellect will rebel and fight against the mantra and come up with numerous excuses to hijack the practice. This will cause difficulties. These struggles may even make you feel a little fearful, insecure or lonely. This, too, will pass! Don't give these little dramas any attention. Just persevere, despite all the internal squabbles and noise! When faced with significant challenges, fears or unexpected crises, such as, e.g., relationship break-ups, illness, debts or losses etc., these are the times when you need to use the mantra more than ever, to stop you from falling back into the illusion. That way, if you slide down and fall out of the witness mode, you can quickly climb back up the Reality ladder again. When these relapses happen, it is essential to be kind to yourself. Don't beat yourself up!

With determination, you will master these avalanches, and in time, with perseverance, you will conquer the mind. Then, slowly but surely, it will begin to turn around, accept, and dissolve back into Source: "I am *Brahman, Brahman* I am". With earnestness, the Conviction will appear spontaneously. Never give up, especially during difficult times, when it may feel as if you are wading through mud! Keep reciting the mantra despite all the thoughts and feelings that appear to be assaulting you.

Things appear to get worse before they get better

Dive deep into the ocean. Don't let the choppy seas disturb you. At a few feet below the surface, there is calmness and tranquillity. Hammer yourself with the mantra, until you have accepted your Reality. The more you recite it, the more it will be accepted as your true nature. "I am Ultimate Reality. Ultimate Reality, I am". During the day, make sure you wear your tool belt at all times. If any unwanted thoughts arise, you can immediately take hold of the mantra and use it to hammer and cancel them out.

Be prepared for things to get worse before they get better! It is like spring-cleaning your house – the gathering of dust may smell bad initially, but then shortly after, your home will be spotless. Momentary anger, depressive thoughts, fearful or sad feelings and all sorts of emotional upsets will create an odour, even a big stink! That is to be expected! After all, your tenants have been there for a long time. Don't be surprised if they hurl abuse at you as they leave. You can't politely ask them to, "please leave". That's not going to work! You must use some force to evict them. For example, when unwanted memories arise, go against the tendency to relive the experiences. Instead of chewing the gum over and over as you would usually do, spit that sticky gum away – all of it! You are neither your memories, nor your experiences.

Ignore the thoughts

Your body is like a big house which has served as a container for millions of concepts. Yours is the only house in which they have ever lived! Concentrated, disciplined and regular practice is the only way to remove them. When you concentrate on the concentrator, a melting process occurs that will inevitably lead you to freedom! When problems arise, don't give them the time of day, ignore them and keep going. Expect these disruptions; they happen because of the cleansing, purifying process that is disturbing and unsettling the status quo.

You must be serious and determined about putting an end to your suffering. Continue the practice, until the entire premises are vacated. Ignore all the negative thoughts that arise. Their only intention is to needle, annoy or distract you, so that you will just give up and abandon the practice altogether. Your inner voice says: "Why bother doing this practice? Let's have some fun!" Remember that whenever there is a "Why?", there is an "I". The ego wants everything to go back to the way it was before so that it can return to its comfort zone. Ignore the ego's influences and keep on hammering. Spend as much quality time with yourself as possible, as this is the only way you can know yourself directly. Expose the phantom ego, the pseudo entity. You gave so much attention to the ephemeral, and now it is time to turn your gaze towards Reality, and fix it on that which is permanent, Selfless Self. You fell in love with the impermanent, now, you can fall in love with the permanent!

Guilt

The process of clearing out your old identity will shake your very foundations and bring various issues to the surface, such as guilt, fear, mortality, etc. We have all felt guilty about something or other that we think we may have done. You may feel guilty about something you did in the past which you have been carrying around with you for decades. When these feelings of guilt arise, ask yourself, "Who is guilty?" Remember, there is no doer, therefore, there can be no deed.

Who is guilty? You are not guilty at all. You became a victim of society's thoughts and feelings, a victim of your dream, a victim of alleged wrongdoings. And in a particular dream, you were maybe crying, ashamed and upset of some so-called misconduct, or God forbid... a "sin" which you believed you had committed. The only crime you are guilty of is in wrongly thinking that you are nothing more than a human being. You are the Ultimate Reality. You are not a human being - therefore, you are not guilty. It is a great shame to accept that which you are not. There is only one "sin", and that is to keep on crying and suffering instead of realizing that this life is all just a dream!

Challenges

Don't be put off by fear either, or by any other illusory feelings that may arise throughout your practice, as they will only distract and throw you off course. Keep focussing on the main task at hand, establishing Reality and hammering illusion. When disturbing thoughts and feelings emerge, you should not give them too much attention. Be like the wind that blows the clouds away, letting them float past without even focussing on them. If you give them attention, they will only get bigger and bigger and gather more power. You don't want the clouds to turn into massive thunderstorms! Let them go! Keep your attention at Source. Recite the mantra with determination, and you will not be drawn in or pulled down, by any kind of illusion.

When you identified with the body, you became embroiled in body-based knowledge. But now, you are peeling away these layers of illusory thoughts, from the gross to the subtle level. When you are no longer feeding the thoughts, but instead starving them of your attention, you will begin to live more freely. When they have all dissolved, you will feel the difference.

You were never in bondage; you have always been free. You are whole and perfect; you have always been complete and perfect. There was just something in the way that was blocking you from knowing this. It was body-based knowledge. But now that the dawn is breaking, all the imaginary layers that once obscured your Presence are dissolving!

Chapter 26.
Stop Clinging!

Every creature struggles to survive. When you identified with the body, you held onto it tightly because you feared death. It is the same for all creatures whether great or small. The Spirit-Presence has become attached to the body-form. Spirit, the principle behind life, has grown very fond of the body-form, to the extent that it will hold on tightly to life, whatever the circumstances! Who wants to live forever? Every living being! We will cling to life at all costs because of our strong attachment to the body-form.

When your default setting is the body-mind, you dread the thought of extinction, of giving up everything you know and love. However, when you change your settings to Ultimate Reality that is birthless and deathless, freedom and abundance are yours. If you undergo this process with trust and determination, you will be liberated from your imagined limitations.

These Teachings and Practices will prepare you well and ensure that when your time comes to leave the body, it will be a very happy event. Keep up the practice and get to know yourself more deeply. Every moment in your life is very precious, never to be repeated. Now is the time to discover your true, immortal nature and to know first-hand that there is no death. There is nothing to fear because you are no one. Who is afraid? You are unborn.

Root out all fear!

Don't let the jaws of death gobble you up. What is the cause of fear? What is the root of fear? It is a big fear of death. But who is going to die? The body will expire, that's all. You are not going to die. You know there is no death. Death is a concept! Death is a ghost! Face this phantom now, otherwise, fear will paralyze you on your deathbed! Death is nothing but an idea. However, to know and believe this intellectually is not enough. It needs to be fully absorbed. Even when we know, "I am not the body", there might still be some kind of deep-rooted fear around us which we have overlooked. Examine yourself and probe deeply! Some sort of dread may still be lurking in the background: subtle worries or anxieties. Make sure your Conviction is not just skin deep!

No one dies and no one is born. One year, two years, fifty years, eighty, ninety years are the concepts related to the material body. You are not that. You are like the ageless sky. You are not subject to poverty, illness, mid-life crises, etc. For many, when they are nearing the end of their bodily life, what often happens is that their fears suddenly intensify. But if you realize the body is not your identity, then fear will no longer haunt you. There is no "I" in the sky. Your Presence is just like the sky which has no fear.

Be serious! Take your Reality on board! Hammer the ego until you have lost all confidence in, "I am somebody", which is the root of all your problems and the cause of all your grief.

Practice, practice, practice, and then, slowly, but surely, there will be the realization of your Reality as Ultimate Truth. After Conviction, you will no longer fear death because you will know deep down, at the core of your being, that you are unborn.

Death of the body is certain

There is no escape from the concept of death. The idea of death is a persistent companion that creeps up on you slowly but surely, guaranteed to perpetuate fear. If, however, you are truly established in your Reality, you will witness the body ageing, knowing that you do not age!

Live and act according to Ultimate Reality, and avoid falling into fearful illusion again. When you know yourself perfectly, your fears around death will drop off, spontaneously.

This body does not belong to you. If you develop a health problem, then, of course, go and check it out with the doctor. However, at the same time, because you know that you are not the body, you will not be overly concerned about your problems. You will not buy into them because you know that whatever appears to be happening is happening to the body alone; it is not happening to you.

Afraid of a mugging

Life can be lived free from fear, without any anxiety or stress. Why do we fear? Because we are attached to the body-form. Suppose you had a wad of cash in your pocket. When you go out, you might be anxious about getting mugged. You look around you nervously, with your hands pushed tightly, in your pockets. You are afraid that someone might rob you.

Conversely, if you had nothing in your pockets, you would be out walking at ease with your arms relaxed by your side. You are fearful because of your identification with the body and all its attachments. The truth is that you are no-thing, and you have no-thing. Be naked, unattached, and live like that!

As long as you still believe that you are somebody, this egotistic knowledge will continue to cause you problems and conflicts. If you lack the necessary commitment to the practice, then this egotistic knowledge will perpetuate the dream, and in turn, perpetuate your illusory suffering. These sticky concepts that have been around you for so long must be unstuck. Be brave! Let all your concepts melt and place yourself prior to beingness. Let go of all that is familiar and just be as you are. Be Selfless Self! Move out of your comfort zone. Break through the barriers and the old paradigms of duality and separation. You know you are not that!

Hope

At some point in our lives, we all say: "One day, I will do this", or "One day, I will do that": fulfil my hopes and dreams, travel around the world or learn a new skill, etc. But there is no such thing as hope. Hope is another concept that serves to keep you living in the future. (Hope is faith without evidence. Master the practice, and you will have/be the evidence.) Taste Reality, take a bite! Give this process time to work. Give it a chance!

You are Presence, Spirit, the Force, the Power, the Principle, the Supreme, the Absolute, that animates everything. You are that immaterial force that gives the body, life, energy and power. You are that vital Essence.

There is an inbuilt yearning in the heart, a hunger to know the infinite. Look within for the permanent, the Ultimate, your Essence. Listen to your Beloved Source! When death comes to the body, all your worldly achievements and illusory assets, will be swept away like dust. Don't waste a minute longer, accumulating more, and planning for some hopeful future. Rid yourself of all the concepts you carry around with you: the past, the future and the present! Love the permanent!

You are awesome!

Your life should be and will be fearless when the ego vanishes completely! Theoretical or literal knowledge is unhelpful. Theoretical knowledge is not useful because it is limited knowledge. You are not limited, but great, awesome, unlimited! You are a giant! You are Almighty! Therefore, find your Greatness! Self-discover and uncover your innate, infinite knowledge.

Just reading and hearing this knowledge has the power to convince you. Reinforce it by convincing yourself at the same time. Convince yourself that you are not the body. That will make you fearless and prepare you to face any problem with full strength and turbo power. It will prepare you for the date when your food-body expires, like the labels on our food cans. Be ready to face the concept of death today, not tomorrow! Be brave!

Emptiness is spaciousness

This whole practice is a potent cocktail that will lead to Self-knowledge and Spontaneous Conviction. Eventually, when you are free of all the illusory concepts, there will be emptiness. That emptiness is not some kind of abyss or void but a vast spaciousness, full of bliss, joy, smiles and laughter. Looking back, you will see the absurdity of your former body-mind perspective, and laugh to yourself at how ridiculous it all was! And, your happiness and humour will spread contagiously to all those around you!

You may wonder if after Conviction you will be able to function as before. Yes, you will, absolutely, with only one difference: There will be a kind of detachment, but at the same time, you will function spontaneously, attending to everything that needs attention! What is it going to be like when all the body-based knowledge has gone? When you are empty of all the illusion, your cup "will runneth over", filling you with happiness. Don't worry! Rest assured!

Once the noise that was coming from the mind finally stops, and the pseudo ego has well and truly crumbled, immense peace will start to flow, and an abundance of causeless happiness. This joy and peace are streaming from your Source, from the bottomless bottom of Reality. Now you will be able to hear the silence within. This new experience, will fill you with the desire to be quiet, and remain silent for some time, just to be, to listen.

At first, the peace will be intermittent, and then, with regular practice, you will experience it for longer durations. You feel good, a little high, and occasionally, even ecstatic. You don't know why, but whatever it is, you want to experience it some more. Little by little, you are finding your identity. You are on your way Home to your Beloved.

At Bootcamp, you are receiving intensive training that will eventually burst your gigantic balloon of concepts. To establish you deeper in your Reality, we shall now use the tool of Meditation.

Chapter 27.
Meditation

The word "meditation" is a big turn-off for many of us. Why? Because it carries numerous negative connotations such as effort, seriousness, discipline, boredom, duty and a heavy vibe, generally. This perception arises from the misunderstanding that we must do and endure some kind of unpleasant activity, as we wear our meditation straitjackets for half an hour, often without any benefits, while impatiently waiting on the minute hand to tell us our time is up! Then we enthusiastically remove our straitjackets, and get back somewhat too eagerly, to the world and its stimuli!

Meditation does not mean identifying with the body, being aware of the body, or feeling whatever sensations are going on in the body. You are not meditating with body consciousness, nor are you using mindfulness, but you are instead meditating without the feeling of the body being there. You are meditating as Presence on Presence. In other words, you are meditating on what you are: the "invisible meditator", or, that Presence that knows you are meditating.

"Oh no, not meditation!" we often exclaim, based on our brief and disappointing encounters with it in the past. But meditation is not something that we do; it is not an activity, but a way of being, that's neither heavy nor serious. On the contrary, it is light, fun and free because it is our natural, thoughtless, stateless, empty, invisible, silent Reality. Abiding in our true nature can be experienced as a gentle stream of flowing grace.

You are not the body or the mind, but unborn, therefore, learn to stay dedicated and loyal to that Stateless State. Live as that invisible Presence.

Just a way of life

Now that you have been weeding out some of the troublesome concepts using Self-enquiry and the Mantra, a greater space has opened up for you to dwell on your Reality. Let's start with basic meditation, which means being still and continuously churning the knowledge of your Reality. Meditating on your true nature will deepen your understanding, enabling you to dwell as your natural state, in that field of Reality. How do you do that? For example, contemplate the truth of "I am Ultimate Reality!" What does it mean? What are the implications? Ponder this! There is only one Reality and you are that Reality. If everything is that Reality, that means everything is within you. Ponder this! Let that truth touch your heart!

Alternatively, you can practice churning the powerful truth: "I am prior to beingness", or "I am unborn". Calmly reflect on your true identity, that Stateless State before beingness, in this way: "I exist! I have always existed, but not as a body-mind. How was I?" Meditating like this draws you closer to your unidentified identity. Here, you are not looking for answers, but instead, tapping into your transcendent nature, your Source, and bathing in that sacred atmosphere, that river of Light.

At the advanced stage, when there is nothing left to dwell upon - because the gap between knowing and being has been bridged, you will be established in your natural state. When this happens, your efforts will no longer be needed

Indwelling 24/7

Meditation in the real sense is not something you can do; it is synonymous with what you are. When knowing and being are one, only then, is real abidance possible, day and night, night and day, in that unlimited Self that you are.

For now, practice meditation: remembering and dwelling on your true identity 24/7 and keeping the focus of your attention on the Source. Don't see it as some twenty to thirty-minute slot or compartmentalized section of your life, where you must remain in a certain uncomfortable *asana* pose. With a quiet, determined passion for finding out who you are, concentrate on your Essence, your Reality. Stay with your Reality at all times. With practice, meditation will become a way of spontaneously living life as you are in your true Essence, at one with the Source that is your Reality.

Your identity is before thought. It follows, therefore, that you do not have any connection to the thoughts.

Don't identify with them! Just let whatever thoughts arise, come and go, without giving them any attention. They are of no interest to you. Using this kind of meditation reduces the thoughts, resulting in the re-establishment of your innate, pure, unblemished, untainted, changeless Reality, centre stage.

Stand at the bank of the river

Don't involve yourself in any thought processes. Why would you, when you have nothing to do with that! You are nothing to do with that. You are the witness that is always standing at the bank of the river. You are not flowing with the thoughts, but letting them pass by like a meandering river. Don't take delivery of them. Don't be upset by them. Don't judge them! There is one exception to this guidance which has to do with specific, recurring thoughts. Because of their nagging presence, they are guaranteed to interfere with your meditation. You must deal with this baggage - whatever issues they may be - and give them your attention. Face these pesty ghosts head-on, and get rid of them once and for all. Otherwise, they will continue to inhibit your progress.

Meditation means being alert, naturally alert, naturally at one with your nature. When your attention is firmly established in Selfless Self, when your default setting is "Selfless Self", the thoughts diminish. Living life in this way as "Thoughtless Reality", is like, spontaneously, gliding through space, free of thoughts, concepts, feelings, or anything else that is sticking to you. If you become aware of something sticking to you, it means you have been sucked back into the quicksand of the mind. And when this happens, the spontaneous, free-flowing energy is interrupted and comes to a sudden halt.

Self-attentiveness

Meditation is non-dual. It is not a subject meditating on an object, but inherent silence. You are the Light that is behind everything. The practice involves staying in, and as, that Light that you are. After some training, the meditation will happen spontaneously and be as natural as breathing. Meditation means being firmly rooted at the very core of your being – your divine headquarters - and operating from there, with what can be described as a spontaneous love of the infinite. When you stay in your Reality zone, you function from your natural home allowing the fragrance of Selfless Self to permeate with spontaneous happiness, peace, and bliss.

Learning to live in the illusory world without falling into its many traps comes with training. Don't make any excuses like saying you do not have a meditation room and therefore, you can't meditate! A meditation room is not essential! Meditate! Don't procrastinate! Practice staying as the neutral witness, keeping your attention focussed on the "Seer", instead of, on the "seen". Stay with the Source instead of the world. And when your attention is drawn away from the Source, gently bring it back. Rein it in as soon as you catch yourself straying from Self-attentiveness.

Once that meditative, Stateless State, is established, it will always be there, no matter where you are or what may be going on around you. In time, everything will be calm, peaceful and silent. You will not be disturbed or perturbed by anything, but blissfully dwelling in that inner silence and stillness of Oneness. With progress, that sense of Oneness will grow and extend until it fills your entire existence. With a blissful feeling that the body is the whole universe, and the universe is within you, that transcendent love will begin to spread, and you will see yourself in "others".

Lapses

Giving too much time to the world, and only twenty minutes to meditation will not work. Especially at the start of your practice, you need to be alert to your nature from morning till night. Throughout the day, when you are distracted and involuntarily get drawn back into thought-forms, you need to train yourself to remember your identity instantly, so that you can bring the focus of attention back to Source. These lapses will continue until you have mastered the practice. Just don't give yourself a hard time over it. If you falter, bounce back a.s.a.p. Don't linger on perceived failures! Keep going forward! Everything comes to those who sweat! The practice will soon become part of your daily routine which you will find not only effortless, but fulfilling.

Establish Reality

When you first begin the practice, you will need to force yourself to remember at all times, that you are not the body. But later on, you will not have to make any effort at all because you will know! The Conviction will grow, first of all, intellectually, and then, spontaneously. When you have learned the art of meditation, you will live spontaneously as your true nature, as your natural state.

Apart from Self-enquiry, reciting a mantra and meditation, another handy tool that will help establish Reality within you is singing/chanting and listening to kirtans. All these tools are needed to weaken the mind's force, and reduce the traffic of thoughts. You can't be thinking when you are otherwise engaged.

Chapter 28.
Kirtan

We are all familiar with music's power and its transforming, transporting properties. Music is a medium for all kinds of expression, even catharsis. We relax, share, make love to, sing and dance to music. It can lift our mood, soothe and iron out uncomfortable feelings and de-stress us. This universal language of the heart that unifies and elevates us has a mysterious, quickening effect that sometimes makes us spontaneously burst into song and dance. Our hearts respond to music, beating to the rhythm, losing ourselves in it and becoming one with the music - all of which helps us forget about ourselves and our problems.

For those who have grown disillusioned with the music scene, having had a gullet full of popular, inane, emotional songs, there is an alternative. An increasing number of people have turned to "new age" music, and are now listening or singing along to kirtans.

Kirtans are devotional songs set to music. Artists such as Krishna Das, Deva Premal, Jai Uttal, and Snatam Kaur (from the Sikh tradition) to mention a few, attract large crowds to their kirtan concerts.

Jai Uttal, an American, Grammy award, sacred music composer and kirtan singer, says: "Soulful music and singing have always had a healing effect on listeners... in combination with the ancient yoga science of mantra chanting, this soulful music uplifts and heals broken hearts, brings calm to the most anxious minds and escorts us to divine realms".

Kirtan – the new Mindfulness

Just as "Mindfulness" became a buzzword over a decade or so ago, "Kirtan" is now heading in the same direction. We are now witnessing a new movement spreading across the world. Kirtan is growing in popularity, perhaps because many people find it easier and more enjoyable than Mindfulness, as it does not require any concentration or focus to find inner peace. Kirtan takes you out of the mind, whereas pop music is 100% egoic! Another bonus is that it is not solely a solitary practice - for which you have to find the motivation - but can be a shared, uplifting, collective experience. Kirtan music is one way of unifying, being part of, and sharing our Universal Divinity.

"My Sweet Lord"

The late George Harrison, a member of "The Beatles" group had the same vision in the 1960s and 1970s. He was looking for ways by which everyone - irrespective of their beliefs - could share, relate to, and experience Oneness. This vision inspired him to write *My Sweet Lord*, released in 1970 which topped the music charts. In this song, Harrison alternated the chorus line of "*Hallelujah*" with "*Hare Krishna*". (*Hallelujah* means

"Praise to God", while *"Hare Krishna"* means "Praise to Krishna, the Supreme Reality".) He managed to hoodwink the listeners who were only too happy to sing along to the catchy melody, without even noticing the *"Hare Krishna's"*!

Transcendence

These days, the same transcendent experience of Oneness or Universal Divinity, can be felt powerfully and beautifully at Jahnavi Mataji's popular kirtan concerts. Jahnavi was brought up by her Hare Krishna, devotee parents in Bhaktivedanta Manor, U.K., purchased by George Harrison.   Coincidentally, Jahnavi's name is "Harrison"; however, they are unrelated!

Using her stirring and angelic voice, Jahnavi chants many different mantras, including the *"Hare Krishna"* mantra. The sound of the mantra has a sacred vibration. When it is chanted over and over again, it has the effect of raising our vibrations. Not only do these sung mantras make us feel more alive, but they also stir something within us that compels us to sing, move, and dance.

Every year, Kirtan events which are open to all take place worldwide. The atmosphere at these sacred music festivals is similar to such gatherings as the Glastonbury Festival in the U.K., with one difference, the participants get high, not from listening to bands playing or drink and drugs, but from the chanting of divine names!

From head to heart

Singing or chanting mantras in Sanskrit has touched a new audience in the West. The understanding is that if you chant a divine name then these sound vibrations will enable you to experience communion or Oneness with your Beloved Source. Kirtans are a call-and-response style of chant. The lead singer sings a mantra first and then the listener responds, by repeating the same mantra.

The chanting of various divine names such as Bhagavan, (Lord), Krishna, Saraswati, (the Goddess of Knowledge), Ganesha, (the Elephant God), Hanuman, (the Monkey God), etc. - with the help of various melodies - is a powerful tool that puts you in touch with the "One, Indwelling Presence", that one Reality that is within us all.

Kirtan is devotional singing from the heart. When you are involved in kirtans, the mind quietens down. Suddenly, those unhappy or sad emotions you may have been feeling, disappear as if by magic! The vibrations' ecstatic power fills our whole being, cleansing, showering, pouring, and saturating our hearts with happiness. In a somewhat mysterious, fast and effective way, the transcendent quality of chanting bypasses the mind. It connects us to our divinity, to the one Source - whether you are listening to the artist-musician, CC White singing soul kirtan, MC Yogi rapping kirtan, or Krishna Das's dulcet tones!

Spreading the love

Krishna Das is one of the most popular kirtan singers in the West. He explains: "It is sustenance food for that living Presence within you. The kirtan experience is enjoyable as the mantras work like medicine effectively, dissolving the ego - unbeknown to most of the participating audience. These kirtans touch the living Presence, or Spirit so that for even just a few hours, there is an experience of interconnectedness - of our one Essence. The vibrations have a power that gets under your skin."

Trance-like celebration

Deva Premal and Miten are, in their own words, "modern nomads on a mission to share with humanity the medicine of mantra... where music is not an ego-driven performance, but rather a portal to contemplation, inner peace and heart-centred connection".

Singing, chanting, or simply listening to kirtans is not only a beautiful experience, but a powerful tool. This activity offers a distraction for the mind, while at the same time taking you to a sacred place, where the heart opens and experiences deepening peace, love and gratitude. Chanting is enchanting! All and all, it is a blissful experience!

When you are singing, the thoughts are absent! The influence of devotional singing has the power to lift the

Spirit and create a happy atmosphere. It is a celebration of Selfless Self, a celebration of "That" through which you know yourself! It touches and soothes the heart, bringing much longed-for rest and peace. Singing is an appealing tool because it is simple, free and available to all. Anyone can chant and reap the benefits without the need to think or understand what they are chanting. As the repetition of a mantra continues and connects you to your power, you are somehow mysteriously taken into a kind of trance-like, celebratory state.

When you don't give the mind attention but bypass it instead, there is the transcendence of the little self. Communion takes place with that greatness in you that is Selfless Self, your Beloved - call it what you will! Chanting heals and purifies the heart so that we become receptacles of that pure love, that Presence within all of us. As you repeat the names and go deeper and deeper, you can feel that connection with Source and experience its perfume: joy, bliss, peace, ecstasy and love.

Chapter 29.
Singing in the Temple of the Heart

Kirtans are love songs to ourselves. They create an atmosphere of festivity and spontaneous celebration. Chanting kirtans is like a powerful, invigorating tonic that stirs, elevates and inspires. As the chanting puts us in touch with our true nature and the vibrations sink effortlessly into our hearts, all our problems seem to be miraculously forgotten - at least, for a little while!

When, for example, we sing *"Jaya Bhagavan"* ("Victory to the Lord"), or "Hail to that one divine essence in all", we are bowing to the One Presence within us, the "Lord" within us. There is no duality here. You are what you are praising. You are worshipping, honouring and celebrating the miracle of your existence. Our *Hallelujah's, Hare Krishna's, Jaya Bhagavan's* or *Jai Guru's* are not expressions of worshipping an external God or Deity because there is only one Reality, and you are That!

You are that Presence, that Selfless Self, that Inner Guru you are singing to, singing about, and for want of a better word, that you are "worshipping". Here, the illusory triad of worship, worshipper and worshipped, are, of course, one and the same. You are all three in one! With Conviction, you are giving praise to yourself – High 5's to Selfless Self. You are filled with gratitude, love and pure joy because you know everything is within you. And not only that, you wish to express your thanks and humility. In other words, you are blessing yourself in recognition of the supreme opportunity you have been given to know yourself! Kirtans celebrate your Selfless Self. They plug you into your Source. When the sound and vibrations grip and transport you, the "mind" is wiped out.

Spontaneous happiness

As you are singing or chanting and immersed in these vibrations, that energy refreshes and re-connects you to your expansive Reality. You lose yourself in the vast ocean of bliss! Presence responds to the uplifting vibrations and keeps the heart soft, open and loving.

If you have ever attended a "Krishna Das" concert, you will have witnessed first-hand, the powerful, magical energy sweeping through the venue. From the young to the elderly, the subdued, to the naturally open-hearted, one by one, like tall, smiling sunflowers sprouting every second, you will have observed how each and everyone got up from their seats and joined in the chanting. Even the most reticent and reluctant ones felt compelled to join in, as if overcome by some power greater than themselves, which is, in fact, what's happening.

It is a joy to see so many faces exuding happiness, experiencing that interconnectedness, unity and oneness and spreading the love! Carried away in a kind of ecstatic trance, along with resounding clapping, the transformational power of kirtan can be experienced as a spontaneous healing of the collective!

Bewildered listeners often comment in response to "Kirtan YouTube" videos. Most of them say they don't know why, or how, but their mood changes when they listen to certain kirtans – ranging from laughter to contentment, to tears of joy. Even though they do not know how they work, they use them as therapeutic tools to get them through the day, or to help them relax at night. Whatever may or may not be happening, it is evident that kirtan has the power to attune you to your Heart and put you in touch with that something beyond the known, the transcendent! Kirtan singer, Gaura Vani, describes kirtan as timeless: "It is the Song of the Soul, running like an underground river in all traditions".

Don't like Kirtan?

Sing, chant or listen to kirtan, morning, noon and night. This activity will keep you in the happy zone! If kirtan does not appeal to you, there are many *bhajans* (devotional songs) that you can listen to, or numerous soft, elevating, stirring sounds of your choosing. Any musical medium that opens the heart and keeps it open will do! There is a wide variety of music online such as World Music, mood-changing/lifting music and meditative music, classical pieces, Gregorian/Tibetan chanting , choral / hymnal music , Native American music, instrumental, space music, Vangelis, etc. (With instrumental music , the egoic mind does not get involved with concepts such as human dramas or loss, past, present or future!) As long as the music circumvents the mind and touches your heart, it will work and have the desired effect!

At Bootcamp, we employ all these complimentary tools to dissolve the ego and the illusory concepts. Singing or chanting opens the heart and keeps it open so that the knowledge of your Reality can be absorbed more easily. Most importantly, devotional singing brings Self-knowledge to life, preventing it from becoming dry, dusty or stale. When the knowledge is fuelled with devotion and gratitude, it enters every cell of our being, transforming it into a flowing, living, loving, practical experience.

Shielded

You are Ultimate Truth. You are unborn. The body-form is the medium through which you can know yourself. When you use it for this purpose, all your insecurities and fears will be removed. The mind will no longer create any fear. All of that will be history! You will live life happily, lovingly, wisely! Apply this knowledge! Practice the techniques! Meditate! Listen only to your inner voice. Keep it all simple. Remember what you are at all times, until you no longer need to remember! We have built many walls around us, conceptual walls. There are no walls. You are like the sky, free from an "I". You are free! Let go of your past dramas, traumas, stories, chaos. Let it all unfold! Trust the process 100%!

You now have a protective shield around you. It is the deepening Conviction of your true nature. This knowledge is the armour that immures you from any challenging issues and attacks that may come your way. You were affected by worldly influences in the past, whereas now, these will simply bounce off you! You are no longer a stray dog looking for scraps in the world, but a divine current that is endlessly flowing in and through, everything.

Your prescription

All four practices: Self-enquiry, Mantra recitation, Meditation and Kirtan, have the effect of disidentifying you from the illusory thinker and thoughts and establishing you in your Truth, in your Reality. Use the tool of Self-enquiry, to find out what you are not. Use the Mantra to erase illusion and establish your Reality. Use Meditation to stay with Source 24/7. And finally, use the tool of Kirtan to oil the knowledge, drown the thoughts in vibration/song and at the same time, to open the heart and keep it open. Kirtan helps the knowledge to flow. Now you have your prescription! Don't just read it. Follow it as prescribed, carefully!

After graduating from Bootcamp, remember to wear your tool belt at all times. You never know when another calamity may come your way. But now you know that when it does, you will be prepared! You will be fully equipped and fully protected!

You have been prescribed the Ultimate Medicine that will lead you to the Altar!

Part Five: The Engagement

"My Beloved grows right out of my own heart. How much more union can there be?" Rumi

Chapter 30.
Drawing Closer to the One

When you absorb the Truth of who you are, it will stir, move and touch your heart deeply, compelling you to find out more about your Reality. This forceful, magnetic pull is like that unforgettable feeling of falling in love with your perfect match.

When you experience a taste of the peace and happiness that this practical knowledge brings, it opens your heart and quickens your longing for fulfilment. This drive that propels you forward feels like magical energy, a divine light beckoning you like a lover, drawing you closer and closer.

In that field of Reality, you are nourished from within. As the light shines and illuminates the darkness, it removes all the ignorance. At this juncture, you have little interest in anything else, except the desire to be with your Beloved Source, to taste the sweetness of Home and enjoy the bliss. Non-dual love means engaging with your Beloved Source, the very Heart and Core of your Being.

Sweet offerings

When the Source is calling you back Home, first of all, you need to remove the obstacles that are standing in the way and keeping you apart from the Source. These obstacles come from the mind with all its accumulated concepts, emotions, memories and attachments. When the Light of light shines, beckoning you forward with priceless, irresistible, sweet offerings, you have no choice but to get rid of your former attachments, so that you can be truly at peace, Home at last, with the One! You feel compelled to know, compelled to touch that sacred ground of your Being.

Engage with your beloved

The process of falling in love, engagement and marriage is a helpful analogy for the spiritual journey. When you meet your dream partner in this dream world, you feel a strong and indescribable attraction at play: as if you see a shining light in him, and he sees that same light in you. When you are together, it feels so right, that you have absolutely no doubt you want to be with him forever.

In his arms is where you belong; it is where you are nourished, cared for, protected, and fulfilled. In his presence, you feel free and invincible. With him, there are no pressures to be the "glamour queen" or pretend to be something you are not. You can forget about all your issues and insecurities because he accepts and loves you unconditionally, just the way you are! Finding him is beyond your wildest dreams! You can be as you are; he can be as he is, and when you are together, something magical happens, something mystical takes place, as if "two" merge into one! You are meant for each other and cannot wait to be engaged!

Similarly, as you engage with the practice and ascend spiritually, you become aware of an energetic force, a magnetic pull that is drawing you inwards. And as you dive deeper within, you are attracted to a powerful, translucent and shining Light that mysteriously seems to be drawing closer and closer. This Light is your Beloved-Source, your real Home and true Love. You do not doubt that this is it! There is no going back!

The highest, purest and most authentic love is already within you as your Source. The love story with your Selfless Self is the greatest love of all. It is not Whitney Houston's call to "love our self", as mortal human beings, but a clarion call to love our eternal, essential nature.

Now there is the recognition, the absolute knowing that you have glimpsed the Light of your original place, your Source, that Power, Energy and Presence, that is your Beloved One. This divine love affair, mystical romance, or whatever you wish to call it, is the ultimate love affair! It is love loving itself. The centre of your beingness is in love with love!

Tasting love

An engagement means making a commitment to the love of your life and announcing your intentions, either publicly or privately, to marry. You are ready to seal the romance formally. How can you be sure that he is the one? From the overflowing happiness and fulfilment, you experience! When you are together, you can't stop smiling and laughing, and that inherent feeling of separation suddenly vanishes, as if by magic!

When you fall in love, when you have tasted love, it is so sweet that you want to taste it again and again. Love has its own momentum, bringing you closer, taking you higher and higher. When love starts to flow, it continues as it will, spontaneously, paying absolutely no heed to reason! Once "betrothed", you can begin to make the preparations for the big day, so that you can spend the rest of your life with your one and only.

Here in the business of Self-realization, preparation refers to the practice of dissolving all the illusory layers, using the tools you learned at Bootcamp! There can be no wedding, and no final union with your Beloved-Source, until this happens. The merging process is marching towards Oneness, but it cannot merge completely, until the illusory you, the ego-mind, has gone for good!

Body training

The search for Truth is challenging and does not come cheap. You need proper training to realize the Self, and for this, you have your very own personal trainer within you. Be serious! Build your Reality body! Keep at it with the same drive and determination that you apply at the gym to work out and tone your body to stay fit. Grow in strength!

Meditation will regenerate your power, helping you to stand on your own feet and be independent! Don't be a slave to anyone's thoughts and views. Don't listen to second-hand knowledge. Keep climbing the Reality ladder! You are progressing, moving closer and closer to Yoga, that eternal union where the thirsty seeker meets the sought after, and that thirst for Truth is finally and forever, quenched. Yoga means union. It is the end of separation - not just a keep-fit endeavour like the Hatha Yoga most of us are familiar with in the West!

Be driven by one desire only: an intense longing to find out "Who/what am I?" Enter more profoundly into the process and concentrate wholeheartedly, inching closer and closer to Reality, with the realization that you are unfathomable and ineffable.

A one-way ticket to bliss

Be with you! Be with your Presence that is Ultimate. You have a one-way ticket to Bliss! Follow your Bliss!

The divine romance is the supreme romance! Surrender yourself completely and unreservedly. We are all pioneers of this unmapped terrain because our journeys are unique. (There are many paths but only one destination or goal.) Be brave, take a leap and let go of your desires and attachments. When you disentangle yourself from all the illusions, your whole viewpoint, stance and perspective will change. You are the Absolute that has never been blemished or stained by anything because you are immutable and therefore, untouchable. Have complete faith in everything unfolding as it should!

Chapter 31.
Wear your Tool Belt 24/7

Access your tool belt regularly using Self-enquiry, mantra, meditation and kirtan. These tools will give you a robust, reliable and stable base. Make your foundation firm and indestructible so that nothing will penetrate or affect you, absolutely nothing. Make meditation your medication! And don't forget to take your medication 24/7.

Examine yourself! Find out if there are any doubts still lingering and if so, remove them! Self-enquire! Are you still a slave of your anger, fears, hatred, cravings, or greed?   If you don't attend to these issues now, but instead, leave them till the last moment – one never knows when that will be - it will be too late!

As has been said many times before, this is a long dream, a long movie! It is up to you to give it a happy ending.   You   are   the   movie   maker,   the producer/director/star in sole charge of creating it all, including the final scene. It is entirely your call! The movie's end does not depend on anyone else but you. You can either make the transition from the form to the formless, floating gently and blissfully, or with great trepidation, let the hungry Grim Reaper devour you!

Face your imaginary demons now! You know them better than anyone else. Expose all your weaknesses and attachments and drop them! For example, say, you are an   investor   stockpiling   wealth,   remind   yourself repeatedly, that you cannot take your profits with you.

Or if you have a beautiful mansion with spectacular vistas, remind yourself that you cannot take your paradise with you. And what about all your ambitions, accolades, awards and achievements, those countless recognitions of your worldly success and attainments? When your body expires, everything that held any meaning for you becomes meaningless in an instant! Keep reminding yourself!

Realize that you are dreaming in a dream world! Know that your real nest egg is within you! You don't need to give up anything. Just realize that all your possessions and achievements are false. That in itself is sufficient to loosen your ties and stop you from hoarding, so that you no longer lose yourself in a maze of worldly existence. Find out if you are on shaky ground. Be thorough! Make sure nothing remains hidden. Demolish and pull down all your constructs until they are razed to the ground and leave no trace. You came into the world naked and you will leave the world bare. You are prior to body-based knowledge: a vessel, empty of all the learning you picked up from the material world.

Checklist

Find out if there is any stress or fear around you. Don't be afraid of annihilation! You cannot kill what was never there – i.e., an illusion. Are you at peace and completely happy? If not, it means you are not quite there yet! But don't lose heart, just keep on hammering!

A number of you may still be holding onto some crucial discoveries you made in the past, e.g., major turning points in life, or some wonderfully happy, mind-blowing experiences and memories which are still precious to you. You are hesitant about letting these go - but go they must - because these experiences are temporary, time-bound, and therefore, illusory. They may have meant something to you in the past, but now you no longer need them.

The Conviction will not arise unless happiness dissolves hand in hand with unhappiness: all the good and bad memories, pleasure and pain, suffering and non-suffering. You are to let go of all the opposites because they belong to the world of duality. True happiness is causeless. It is your very nature. We are not in the business of "making memories", but unmaking them! Euphoric recall or its opposite is always greatly exaggerated, if not altogether false. Memory is deceptive and gives you a false sense of continuity, serving only to keep you captive as a body-form.

If you have been trying to crack the code of your existence for some time, say for five, ten, or even forty years, it is natural to encounter some resistance. You don't want to let go of everything, for fear that your long period of searching was a waste of time, meaningless, and ultimately, in vain. Forget about that! It is just another trap you have fallen into because you are measuring the years and assessing everything with the mind. Come out of this prison of body-based knowledge! Who is counting the years? Even after twenty, thirty, forty years, many people are still carrying some baggage, searching for truth alongside their unhealthy tendencies, weak spots, and various neuroses. It happens because their base is still an illusory one.

Make sure you are free and fearless! Make absolutely sure there are no shadows still hovering around you. When you know what you are, Be That! Self-knowledge removes all your fears and suffering, enabling you to face the most challenging situations that come your way.

Chapter 32.
Constant, Loving Nurturing

The nectar seed of Truth which has been planted in you, needs to be constantly and lovingly nurtured with regular practice. This nectar plant requires your attention for it to grow. You need to take good care of it by offering and expressing your TLC (tender loving care). Water it, keep it in the light and exercise patience to ensure that it grows into a sturdy, tall and beautiful plant. If you ignore or neglect it, the plant will simply wither and die! But if you tend to it and watch it grow, your affection and love will grow in unison. Take care of your Beloved with love and devotion.

When, as a seeker or aspirant of truth, you catch that first scent - the perfume of the Infinite, you will experience a sense of inner freedom, pure joy, love and stillness. That stillness is saturated with peace and beauty. When this happens, your passionate love for Reality, for the Beloved Source that you are, will spontaneously grow and grow, until you are consumed by that love.

You are devoted to your sports team

Use the practice tools! Nourishing the Spirit is just as important as looking after the body with food, clothing, exercise, bathing, etc. Regular attention to your Presence, to Selfless Self, is essential.

Your devotion is needed. Oh no! Not devotion! Don't be put off by the word! What is devotion? Here we are not talking about a pious, "holy, holy", kind of thing that involves praising and serving an external "God" or "Master". Not at all! Devotion and earnestness mean longing to know your Self perfectly as Selfless Self. It means caring for and loving your Beloved, in the way you care for and love your nearest and dearest, your partner, or best friend. Devotion is Self-attention. The practice of devotion means fixing your attention on your Reality. When this occurs, it shuts down the thought factory, with the effect that the mind stops manufacturing thoughts, and you remain ego-free.

We are all devoted to something or other, at different times in our lives. We are obsessed, often fanatical, about something or someone: sports teams or dramas like *Game of Thrones,* film/novel series like Harry Potter, or a particular music genre, band member, career, pets, political causes, etc.

In the caring profession, the good doctors, nurses and carers are devoted to their patients. They have a natural urge to help and care for them, do what they can, ease their suffering, and improve their lives. Closer to home - if you are devoted to your husband, wife, parents, grandparents or close friends – it is fair to say that there is nothing you would not do for them because you love them.

We don't have to question, or think, even for a moment: "Will we, or will we not look after them?" We are driven by our impulse to care and love. This instinctive force is naturally inbuilt and moves us to express it as love in action.

The Divine Romance

The divine romance is devotion to your Beloved Source through Self-attentiveness. As you look after your Beloved with a heart full of love, you can't help but surrender. You may find yourself spontaneously bowing and blessing yourself. Experiences of sheer wonder, awe and grace can bring you to your knees. You have glimpsed the ground of your being. Non-dual love leads to a merging and union with Selfless Self. As you rediscover the blissful landscape of the Heart, you begin to feel whole again because you have returned to the place of your origin. You are Home, at last!

We have been comparing the process of Self-Realization to an enduring, lasting, loving romance where a relationship leads to an engagement and eventually to marriage. Here the Ultimate Romance experienced and described by many as the "mystical journey" takes place in the cave of your heart, your inner temple. You have found your home, your happy place, where sweet offerings entice you to check in more frequently, and for longer periods, to love-bomb with yourself!

After dating for some time, it is here that you will "pop the question" and become engaged. However, as mentioned before, the marriage will not, and cannot happen, until the pseudo-self's mask is completely removed. This caveat is set in stone: only with total and absolute Conviction of your Ultimate Reality can the "Final Union" occur. It is up to you to make this happen. How? By letting your Beloved Source gobble up, devour and absorb every last, remaining particle of your ego!

Rumi, the great, 13th century Persian, Sufi mystic and poet (described as the "best-selling poet in the U.S.), writes beautifully about the mystical journey: "Love is such a blazing fire which, when it blazes up, burns away everything except the Beloved".

The sculptor

The following illustration from an ancient text simply depicts the process of removing the illusory layers, until what you are, and what you have always been, is revealed - self-evident and shining!

A sculptor is engrossed in her work. After she has hammered a stone structure sufficiently using her skill and precision, she reveals a statue. The figure was already there. It just needed the removal of some of its parts that were surplus to requirements. She had to work hard, smoothing out several sharp edges - the add-ons that had somehow attached themselves to the stone. She knew she had to detach these jagged protrusions as they did not belong there.

Just as the sculptor thought she had taken away all the imperfections, she discovered another badly distorted area in need of attention. Once more, she began to chisel and chip at it with some force. However, despite her efforts, she was unable to dislodge it. This part seemed firmly affixed to the stone, as though it had been stuck on with superglue. However, the sculptor did not give up! She persevered with the job at hand, using her skill, care and one-pointed determination. And eventually, when these "cling-ons" fell away, a beautiful statue was unveiled, revealing the perfect expression of divinity!

Here, you are the sculptor. Your job is to eliminate all the unwanted parts that have no place in perfection. And like the sculptor, you need perseverance, dedication and devotion to chisel out all your imperfections! Reality will only be revealed in all its fullness, wonder and glory when there are no traces left of illusion. When you do away with all the layers of ignorance, you become aware of what you are. And what you are is the same as what you have always been and the same as you will always be!

At this stage in the process you will realize that what you used to take for real was, in fact, illusory! It was only an appearance, like seeing a snake instead of a rope. Before beingness, there was existence, but the body was absent. After the body expires, the body will be missing, but existence will continue, And presently, there is that very same existence. The body is only an appearance.

Eradicate all the add-ons without exception! Strip away the concepts of birth and death, pain and suffering, happiness and sadness – they all belong to the world of duality. Clear out the old ground so that the seeds of Oneness can grow. Be free of all "perceivables" and "conceivables", and with courage, step into the uncharted landscape, that ultimate realm that is timeless and spaceless.

Shining clarity

Sometimes when we need to defragment our computers to free up space, we get a little impatient while waiting for the machine to shut down, and then reboot. You might feel the same impatience and edginess during this transformative, cleansing process, which is virtually erasing all your precious, familiar files. The best way to deal with this discomfort of loosening your attachments is to simply ignore all the unsettling feelings and disturbances of doubt, anxiety or suspicion, that are bubbling up to the surface.

The dark night of the ego will come to an end soon, and when it does, you will see thrilling and inspiring changes. With practice, the traffic of thoughts will reduce considerably. And then, a shining and brilliant clarity will emerge, along with many "AHA", light-bulb moments. Let go of your old, make-believe world. If you trust the process 100%, you will be rewarded 100%. Let this unearthing of illusion unfold!

What is now taking place is a clearing away of the debris of your old life. Let the purifying process happen! It is best not to try and work out what is going on or how? If you are about to have an operation, you will trust the surgeon to do the job. In the same way, let this thorough and complete overhaul take place. Go with the flow!

Chapter 33.
Love Found Love

We have all seen people who are very happy for no apparent reason. They do not depend on external sources or circumstances to be so happy. Nothing bothers them! That is the state! The absolute immensity of your existence will gradually reveal itself like nothing you have ever experienced before. As you tap into your Beloved-Source, you are activating your limitless potential. After a thorough deprogramming, the veil will begin to lift. Make sure you have purged yourself of all your illusory baggage, in readiness for that significant download of your Reality.

When the shift occurs, you will be able to see what has always been there. It is not something new, but you will see it, as if for the very first time. It feels euphoric, like that first kiss with the love of your life. You just know! Your whole being screams "Yes"! You feel exhilarated! You don't need to question whether you have met the one because it is so apparent!

Until then, keep the practice going. Meditate and recite the mantra all the time, until eventually, it continues by itself, spontaneously, automatically, without your knowledge. Slowly, but surely, as Reality is hammered into you, over and over again, the Spontaneous Conviction will arise - that you are not the body-mind complex, but Ultimate Truth. What is Reality? "I am not the body. I was not the body. I will not remain the body."

Keep going forward, removing the old ways of thinking. Keep going deeper!

Sometimes your journey may seem intense – and at times, even turbulent! The process may feel more like a demolition job than a light spring clean. It may feel like you have travelled a very long distance, but you have not travelled at all! There was no journey. Everything is as it has always been and as it will always be. Nothing has changed. The blinkers have been removed and the illusion eradicated. That's all that has occurred. Light found Light. Truth found Truth! Love found Love! You have always been in your original place; you have always been as you are, changeless. The mind that was using all your energy has melted and is now very quiet. You can see and feel a refreshing energy burgeoning. Limitless power is at hand, surging, exploding, and shining bright.

After practising for some time - meditating, Self-enquiring, reciting the mantra, and not letting the thoughts back in - you will finally realize that you are unborn. You will see what you are not. And then this deep understanding will turn into Conviction. You will know that there is something far greater underpinning us all.

What is Spontaneous Conviction? It is not an intellectual conviction. It is living with the non-phenomenal certainty of your true identity at all times. In the past, you identified with the body and lived from that illusory foundation. When you know what you are deep down from direct experience, you will live in, and from, the foundation of Reality.

Now that you do not have the same distractions taking up your space and energy, your refurbished operating system will function at optimal performance level, with hardly any thoughts surfacing. And even when they do arise, they will not disturb you. You will no longer be attracted to worldly things as you used to be because the old scripts and stories have lost their power and are now hollow. You will not be drawn into the games or lose yourself in delusion: world events, politics, etc., ever again, including those hard-wired fantasies. You will stand firm as a witness watching the movie. Eventually, when the "witness" concept has served its purpose, it, too, will fall away.

When you are plugged into the Source, you can almost glimpse your Beloved acting as a conductor of a universal orchestra, overriding any imbalances and ensuring that the grand symphony flows perfectly. By continually dwelling on your Reality, throwing out all the disturbing concepts and staying with, and in, Source, you will be able to identify the unidentified identity that you are.

You will be able to live life freely, without "you" being there. When the egoic you is out of the way, Presence takes over completely, and life is then lived spontaneously. When all the thoughts and concepts related to the body dissolve, the epitome of fearlessness will emerge because there is no longer a "fearful you". And when difficulties arise, you will remain aloof and handle everything calmly. It will be like you are acting in a dream – which, of course, it is! You will keep your head above water at all times. There will not be any anxiety or suffering. Who is suffering? Self-realization is attainable for all!

The door is open

The door to Self-knowledge has opened. It will continue to open more expansively as you engage with Source. Find the answer to "Who am I?" by going to the root, to the base. The root is your Beloved Selfless Self. Rest here quietly and calmly without words, without worlds. Here you will see yourself in full light. The Principle resides here. Beyond that, there is nothing, no-thing, nothing else, nothing more. There is no-thing beyond, (but that nothing is everything). All the strength and power will be yours when this is known and accepted.

You have been given a precious opportunity: the gift of your body, as it is the medium through which you can know yourself. Every moment of your life is sacred and grace-filled! Honour that gift by being with you, 24/7! Keep the company of Selfless Self at all times. Cultivate a precious friendship and discuss everything! Ask questions, share and confide! Remember that your Beloved Source is your best friend, your one and only True Love. You can trust your Beloved-Source 100%. There is no need to fear rejection. Don't hold back! Dissolve in the arms of your Beloved into Oneness, where you are embraced, looked after, and tenderly enveloped by love.

As your journey deepens in intensity and intimacy, you will be filled with love, a love that is becoming increasingly explosive, making you feel like a "walking time bomb of bliss"!

Engage with your Beloved. Go deep, deeper, and still deeper. Let your Truth touch your heart. Let that Truth give you the vision to see Reality, to see your Self, and live as that Self.

Meditation – a turn-on!

After experiencing a taste of the peace, silence and happiness within – an indescribable contentment that overfills your heart - you will want to spend more and more time with your Beloved-Source. After tasting a little nectar, you will no longer look at the practice as a chore, turn-off or a painful duty, as you once did, but quite the opposite. Since finding the drug that will give you permanent Bliss, with no side effects, but deep peace, you will suddenly be filled with a longing to meditate! You have now reached a significant landmark: your perspective has changed! Instead of forcing yourself to meditate, you will now see it as a "turn-on", and eagerly look forward to entering your inner temple frequently.

You have set your intentions, examined everything under a microscope and shared all your secrets. You are sure that you have not overlooked any hidden gremlins that might pounce on you one day.

You have found your Home. You have found your Heart! You have found your secret sanctuary, your happy place, your very own penthouse suite where you can experience the Bliss of stillness. You can't stop smiling and laughing! The Ultimate Romance has finally led to your Engagement.

The darkness of ignorance has, at long last, been removed, giving you light with which to see. That Light is in you! You are betrothed, engaged! Celebrate your engagement to that shining Light, that inextinguishable Love that is the Beloved-Source that you are!

Part Six: Wedded Bliss

*"I once had thousands of desires, but in my one desire
to know You all else melted away." Rumi*

Chapter 34.
The Ultimate Wedding

When at long last you know that your long search has
ended, you will feel like the luckiest being on the planet,
bathed in heavenly grace: an energy that is infinitely
loving, warm and all-encompassing. And as you
experience love's tender caresses and melt into love, you
will know that the love story with yourself is about to
reach its culmination, fulfilling your deepest longing.

The wedding to your Beloved will not take place in
Las Vegas, but much closer to home. The venue is
located in the innermost sanctuary of the Heart! When
you marry your Beloved, you are marrying Selfless Self,
your only true, trusted confidante and friend. Selfless
Self will never let you down, cheat on you, betray or
divorce you. This marriage is eternal. The love of the
Infinite, the Source, whatever you wish to call it, is Self-
love, true love, the highest love, the true meaning of
love. Love loves everything as itself. It is love loving
love, in and through, love. That vast expansive love is
neither sentimental nor fickle; it is impersonal,
changeless and unconditional.

The fire is ablaze

Go deep and deep into your Selfless Self to see all that is within you: Reality that is no-thing, and every-thing. You are on sacred ground - sacred because we cannot speak about it. Truth is beyond "I am Ultimate Reality", beyond everything that we can put into words. It is beyond "Selfless Self", beyond the "Beloved Source", beyond "stillness", and "silence". The Reality that you are will be realized when there is not the slightest trace of ego left.

Now it is in your hands. It is up to you! Forget about all the concepts. Be empty and stay empty! "Empty" means that you are full of Presence. When everything dissolves, the indescribable remains. When the illusory house you once lived in is finally demolished and your previous identity has been permanently erased, what is left is a vast expanse of space, in which "you" are infinitely free. You have been guided back to yourself. The ashes have all blown away and the fire is ablaze!

As you investigate all the ideas you have about yourself, contemplate, reconsider, and clear everything out, you are inching closer and closer to your Reality. When you let go of your self-image and the thoughts become fewer and fewer, you will be able to hear the silence. There is peace. Maybe for the first time in your life you can experience an exquisite, indescribable peace. You don't know what you have found! Even though you cannot describe it, nevertheless, you know it is perfect! When the practice has done its job, and the ego has been truly hammered and smashed to smithereens, Reality emerges.

Destination

You feel so blessed! Once upon a time, you were buried under the ashes. Then you heard the drumbeat of knowledge, devotion and love, and you became one with the beat. The ashes were swept away. The divine spark turned into a flame, and the flame burst into a blazing fire. You have never felt so free. Nowadays you look at everything with different eyes and heightened vision. You never thought it would happen to you. You never thought you would find what you were looking for - the Self you had never lost.

In the arms of the Beloved, all is perfect, simple, flowing, fresh and innocent. You feel free like a playful child again, while at the same time, the business of life is taken care of, spontaneously. You are back Home! In effect, you never left. You just lost your way in the dark.

The process, the knowledge, and the practice are illusory, however, they are essential to remove the primary illusion of "I am somebody". This knowledge has reminded you of your true identity. Now that you know who you are, you have reached your destination. You have always been the destination!

Now that you have been restored to your fountainhead, your original glory - the way you are prior to beingness, you know who you are. You have unravelled the most incredible secret: the secret of your existence. You are, you were, and you will always be free. There was never any bondage, that was all an illusion! You were bound by many concepts and preoccupied with worldly concerns and regrets, but now that you are liberated from yourself, all those imaginary limitations have vanished. Not so long ago, you were covered with layers of packaging and wrappers that were tied securely. Now that you have been unwrapped, the concepts have disappeared and you are unshackled. You know that you are free again, complete and independent. You can see all the blessings around you. Your glass is full to the brim! You can now live happily ever after like in the fairy stories, however, this is not a fairy story, but your Reality, your Truth, Liberation!

Lighthouse

You have found your happy home. The foundations of this palatial mansion are solid. Your marital home was built to last, not for just one hundred years or so, but for eternity. Your home is not like any other home in which you have lived. This house is a house of light pouring out bliss, joy and laughter. It is a Lighthouse built for "me-time". In this sacred space where you are connected to your Divine Source, you can pamper your Spirit. "Me-time" is "Alone" time, or, more accurately, "All-One" time. Here you are bathed in light, happiness, peace and love. In your Lighthouse, you receive emissions of grace: your heart enjoys oneness with the

Beloved, experiencing absolute stillness in the depths of your being.

Everything is Ultimate Reality

The process you have undergone is like the children's board game of "Snakes and Ladders". It started with a descent, the hammering of the ego and the beheading of King Ego; it ended with an ascent, the enthronement of Queen Bliss and Self-Realization. First of all, we learned that everything is an illusion, including the world, so we slid down the snake to the very bottom, uncovering and uprooting all the layers of illusion, until we unearthed our foundations, and touched our natural Source, Ultimate Reality. Secondly, we investigated ourselves to find out who we are, and with practice, were established in that Ultimate Reality. Then finally, we climbed to the top of the ladder, from which we can now see the same vista from a different perspective. Following this shift in perception, everything is renewed, refreshed, and seen with amazing clarity. The world is now seen as a reflection of that one Ultimate Reality.

What has been presented here is your eternal Truth. You are the all-pervading, unchanging, Self-Existent and Self-Luminous Absolute! Let these words touch you deeply, then drop them. You are ineffable. You mustn't store anything! Let your truth be impressed deep within your core and allow it to flourish in your heart. You have finally realized the Truth: You are unborn! The body and all you took yourself to be is not your identity.

What makes this knowledge different from the rest? It has the power to remove illusory knowledge and replace it with direct knowledge of your Reality! These absolute teachings are non-intellectual. They transcend knowledge effectively because they are before and beyond knowledge!

These teachings take us back to our roots, "prior to beingness", clearing out the layers of body-based knowledge. They perform a total demolition job on illusion, thus bringing the search to a complete stop. You were free. You are free. You will always be free. Life will unfold, simply and spontaneously, now that there is no longer any interference from the ego. Dive in! Let your innate knowledge flow! Keep plunging into your most incredible adventure ever! Enjoy!

Chapter 35.
"Happy Ever After"

Absorb this knowledge! Drink it all in! It is firewater! You could say it is the elixir of life because by imbibing this nectar, the Reality of your eternal nature is revealed, which, in turn, enables you to live happily ever after. Now that you know the secret of your life, the nectar will intoxicate you as it seeps into every cell of your being. Here, intoxicated means that you are absorbed in your world of bliss. Drink! You are the stimulant. You will not need any other stimulant because you do not have any desires. For what? You will be blissed out on silence, love and peace, tuned into one channel only - your happiness channel. Or "God's" high frequency, off-the-scale channel – which as we know by now - are both the same! The 14th century, German mystic, Meister Eckhart stated: "The eye through which I see God is the same eye through which God sees me".

There is one message, one fundamental principle alone: "Except for your Selfless Self; there is no God". The term "God" does not exist outside of you and neither does "happiness". You cannot find them anywhere else, except within you. No one told you it was an inside job! Now you know that everything is within you! There is nothing else, nothing more.

Altered state

You have heard the message; you have the roadmap. Now it is up to you to make your way. You have been given a jigsaw puzzle with your face on it! All you have to do is fit the pieces together because you know yourself better than anyone else!

After the meltdown of the mind, Reality is accepted. When the knowledge is completely absorbed, there is Self-Realization. And as you relax into being what you are and settling into that altered, Stateless State, life will continue as before, but in a detached manner, with a completely new and fresh perspective. It is still the same old world, but now transformed! There is only One Reality, no polarity! You don't see "good" or "bad", or prefer good over bad. You are free from desire, anger, unhappiness or sadness. You are free from all duality that is the cause of suffering. When you have "seen the Light", you will attend to your worldly duties, minus the old expectations you once had: that the world could, and would, bring you "personal" results. You have transcended all the darkness, unhappiness, and vicissitudes of life. The one who saw herself as a mortal being and thought she was in bondage, has vanished. With dispassion, you no longer experience any desires or losses because absolutely nothing can touch you, let alone stick to you. The ego-less you is like a non-stick frying pan!

You will glide through the movie that is your life, effortlessly attending to those matters that need your attention, before moving on, without looking back, or storing anything! What has changed? Everything is as it was before, except without "you" being there! When you become one with the Final Truth, that is Conviction, Self-Realization, or whatever you wish to call it. When you were a toddler - before any worldly ideas of say, becoming a train driver, athlete or astronaut were implanted in you - you just wanted to continue to be what you were already (without knowing it!) - spontaneous and free! Now, you are that!

Unborn wedded bliss

Remember that all this knowledge is about the "unborn child". It is a vehicle for awakening that provides you with the address you need to reach your destination. On arrival, throw this knowledge away (as you would throw away your used train tickets), including the triads of "knower, known, knowledge", "seer, seen, seeing", etc. Don't hang onto any of it! These teachings have served their purpose, conveying the understanding, that there is nothing but Selfless Self, and that all knowledge is an illusion (including the concepts of "Selfless Self" and "illusion") because you are unborn. They serve as a medium to let you know that ultimately there is nothing to know. The teachings are essential to enable the discernment of the false and to know that: "That" which has seen the false, is not false.

When you give up the ego unconditionally and absolutely, you are not drawn to the same, old attractions and body-related love and affections that belong to the world of duality. You have found your centre, your Source, and as a consequence, spontaneous love of that Infinite Source is soaring by leaps and bounds.

Before awakening from the dream, you felt incomplete. You felt that something was missing, so you searched for a partner to fall in love with: the other half you hoped, would make you feel whole and complete. After awakening, you know that you have always been complete. With this awareness of your actual value, you are no longer looking to "fall in love", but to "rise in love", instead.

Now that you are at the 11th hour, there may be some anxiety around. You wonder if you might end up living like a monk, chanting "OM", wearing saffron robes, shaving your head, or even adopting a new, holy name! Or maybe you are panicking about becoming some kind of hermit, living in complete isolation. Don't worry! Don't be deluded! Adopting any kind of new, outer identity would simply mean that you have taken a big step backwards. That's not going to happen! Fear not!

Relationships will continue. Of course, they will! And they will be even more loving than before because selfish needs no longer drive them. After directly experiencing the knowledge and love of the Self, this communion with our authentic nature, cannot help but overflow into every area of our lives. Our relationships will be based on selfless love rather than ugly neediness which only strangles love. They will be more giving, without the previous expectations we once had, of getting something back. Everything will unfold spontaneously, as a consequence of love flowing from that one pure, unlimited, impersonal Source.

At home with your Beloved

You have arrived at the destination. You have found the missing link. You are the destination. You are Ultimate Truth, Ultimate Reality. Now let go of the words! At long last, you know who you are. You are not in the world, but the world is in you. The world is the spontaneous projection of your Spontaneous Presence. You are formless like space, skylike, everywhere. You are not the body-mind. You are unborn! Get used to the silence. It is in the loving silence that you can scoop up grace, like scoops of divine ice cream!

To recap, we are all part of the same Reality. We are one. We are not separate but interconnected. We are not individuals or persons but one unified Essence. There are no differences or distinctions between us! There are no women, men, or gender of any kind. Neither are there any intelligent beings, nor not so intelligent beings. There are no heterosexual, gay, or asexual beings. There are no believers and non-believers. There are no religions or spirituality. There is no I, no you, no she, no he. You are formless. Your essence is, was, and will always be. You are prior to the body, the mind, the world and the universe. You are prior to everything.

What are the implications of experiencing this knowledge, of knowing yourself as you are? They are immeasurable! An end to suffering, immortality, permanent happiness and peace.

Truth does not change. Whatever changes or passes is time-bound and therefore, temporary. That which passes cannot be the truth. You gave all your attention to the world with its changing concerns. Now you are giving it to your essence, your true nature, your Beloved-Source. You gave your attention to the mutable. Now you are giving it to the immutable, your Ultimate Reality that is nameless.

Chapter 36.
Self-Realization is Not Something New

Self-Realization cannot be something new, i.e., an add-on. What you are looking for has always been within you. It was, is, and will always be. Don't expect something new to happen, since the new cannot be Truth. When the false dissolves, all that is left is that Beloved, silent, living, loving Presence.

All those feelings that you took on, feelings of depression, anxiety, unhappiness, frustration, sadness, etc., came from your acceptance of the imaginary self, the world and your identification with everything in it. Then you changed your view, your perspective. These feelings have now disappeared because the duality has gone. The Conviction arose that everything is within you and nothing and no other, is out there. There is no "myself" and "yourself". There is only Oneness like the sky.

Self-Realization means you have experienced the Conviction, i.e., Self-Knowledge is established. In other words, that Stateless State is permanent. If someone suggests, "You must come and listen to this teacher... he knows it all... he is great!", you will not show the slightest bit of interest or curiosity. Detachment and indifference are signs of Self-Realization! When the Conviction is firmly rooted and established, you will have neither the need, nor the wish to entertain any illusion because you experience your own Self-fulfilment. You are already complete! That is Spontaneous Conviction. There you are, at the last station, the final station, the destination, where all search ends. You have reached the mountain peak!

You cannot grasp the ungraspable

The recipe for Reality has been served to you on a golden platter. Can you accept it totally or are you still looking for further instruction? Maybe you are frustrated because you want to define what you are, take the answer with you, and carry it in a new wrapper! Perhaps you were under the illusion that there is something to know, something to grasp, so that when you had it, you could respond to the question, "Who am I?" with a neat answer. But there is nothing to know. No-thing! You were searching to find the Truth that was already in you all along. Your identity is invisible, nameless, formless, beyond words and worlds.

Throughout the centuries, many seekers have realized the same Truth. We can respect and be guided by the Self-Realized beings, sages, saints and mystics from different parts of the world who have gone before us, e.g., the Buddha, Jesus, Shankaracharya, Ramana Maharshi, Vivekananda, Ramakrishna, Rumi, Kabir, Guru Nanak, Sai Baba of Shirdi, Anandamayi Ma, Yogananda, St. Teresa, St. Therese, the Dalai Lama, Shri Nisargadatta and Shri Ramakant, to name but a very few. After enormous determination, discrimination, meditation, searching and sacrifice, they arrived at the same realization: "*Aham Brahmasmi*" or "*I am That*!". One candle flame lit up another one and then another, spreading the knowledge and waking up the dreamers in many different lands. And not only that, among the many sacred texts, we can be guided by the ancient, classic *Upanishads* which reveal the same Truth, "*Tat Tvam Asi!*": "*That Thou Art!*"

Silent knowing

Where are you at now? Do you have any doubts like: "Are you sure that is everything, all the knowledge? What about "prior to beingness". How is that? " Do you still want more? If this is the case, find out who wants more? You want to understand it better! Who wants to understand?

True freedom comes from knowing that all knowledge is an illusion; absolute freedom comes from knowing that you know nothing. Knowing that you are nothing is liberation. When you know you are nothing, simultaneously, this means you are everything. Find this out for yourself! As the great Master, Shri Nisargadatta Maharaj said: "Love says, 'I am everything'. Wisdom says: 'I am nothing'. Between the two my life flows".

Go deeper and deeper, closer and closer to Selfless Self. All the secrets will be revealed to you through your meditation. Then you will know and understand without words, what has been conveyed here through words. You will see that you are prior to beingness, and "Be

That" - stateless, thoughtless, peaceful, happy, and free – *Sat-chit-ananda*!

Many of us enjoy a long soak in the bath, swimming and sunbathing. Now we can soak in the Divine forever. Our thirst has been well and truly quenched. Golden silence is now thundering! You will know who you are with practice. It is a silent knowing that allows you to rest as Selfless Self and enjoy the sun's rays, as you swim in that eternal, vast sea of serenity.

With complete trust, you surrendered yourself completely! You will never be lonely again! The company is blissful. You cannot keep away. Be devoted to your Beloved. Entering your Heart space is like visiting a beautiful cathedral with stunning celestial vibrations, or an enchanted garden sprinkled with heavenly scents.

Tying the knot

When the ego-knot of illusion which had a stranglehold over you is untied and finally snaps, the original, divine knot is re-tied. It is only now that you are free to marry and enjoy wedded bliss, in blissful union with your Beloved, in Oneness.

The "Ultimate Wedding" is this consecrated marriage. You take your vows seriously. As you make your sacred promise and feel the kiss of the Beloved, your eyes overflow with blissful tears. You can hardly contain the excitement because your longing is fulfilled, at long last!

You can scarcely believe you tied the knot! You are ecstatic, beyond words.

Now cured of your amnesia, there is the understanding that your longing for total fulfilment, did not arise from you, the individual, as you had once thought, but came from the divine spark within you. All along, it was the Divine calling you Home!

You are intoxicated. This is the pinnacle of the Divine Romance! Marrying your Self is the highest love. True Love is Self-Love, Divine Love, Love of the omnipresent Infinite! Some kind of fever has gripped you, or is it madness? Either way, you don't care! You are full to bursting with bliss because there is no longer a "you".

When the *Wedding March* plays, it evokes an overwhelming welling up of love. The melting process that was marching towards Oneness has reached its completion. You have recovered your wholeness. The wedding marks the culmination of the sacred journey. The Union has taken place. You have been restored in your Truth, restored in your Light! Lighter than light, you are "dancing on bubbles"!

When your Infinite Being is realized as none other than "You", it means that the Mantra, *"Aham Brahmasmi"*, has been wholly absorbed. Ultimate Reality is re-established.

Who am I? The question disappeared along with the "i". The "seeker" melted into the "Sought". The Lover, the Beloved and Love are one. However, to keep us humble, it is a natural and beautiful thing to give thanks to the Beloved, spontaneously. Express your gratitude and love and let it flow back to Source. There is no duality in this joyful devotion that celebrates the wonder and miracle that you are.

Be as you are! Relax into that Divine Essence that you have always been. Humbly place your hand on your head and bless your unborn Selfless Self with a smile.

Dizzy with ecstasy, you take to the floor for the first dance. You are the Bride and the Bridegroom, the Lover and the Beloved, entwined in eternal intimacy. This dance is the dance of the sacred marriage that dances and dances forever.

Further Reading

Selfless Self, (2015, pub. Selfless Self Press) Ed. by Ann Shaw, (also available in French, Spanish, Dutch, Japanese, Korean, Greek.)

Be With You, (2016, pub. Selfless Self Press) Ed. by Ann Shaw, (also available in French, Spanish, Dutch, Portuguese.)

Ultimate Truth, (2018, pub. Zen Publications, Mumbai.)

Timeless Years With Shri Ramakant Maharaj 2012 – 2022, (2022, pub. Selfless Self Press) Ann & Charles Shaw.